JAMES HENRY COUSINS

JAMES HENRY COUSINS

A Study of his Works in the Light of

The Theosophical Movement in India and the West

DILIP KUMAR CHATTERJEE

Foreword
Prof. D.K. BARUA

1994
Sharada Publishing House
DELHI - 110052

First Published 1994

ISBN : 81-85616-25-6

Published by
B.L. Bansal
for SHARADA PUBLISHING HOUSE
(Publishers on India's Past and Present)
E-239, Shastri Nagar, Delhi-110052
Phone : 7516539

Laser Typesetting by
Akriti Computers
B-5/98, Paschim Vihar, New Delhi - 110063
Phone : 5587403, 5584110

Printed at:
Raj offset Printers
Ajadpur, Delhi

James Henry Cousins

FOREWORD

My interest in James Henry Cousins sprang from my own research on Edward Carpenter (1844-1929), poet, social reformer and mystic. Cousins was an ardent admirer of Carpenter and visited him at Millthorpe, Sheffield, before he came to India to take up an appointment under Mrs. Anne Besant's Theosophical Society. Carpenter was not a Theosophist but he was held by many among them as their spiritual mentor. Anne Besant herself once told Olive Schreiner, the South African novelist and an early feminist, that whenever she was depressed and doubtful about life she read Carpenter to revivify her spirit.[1]

The Cousinses, James Henry and Margarette, derived much inspiration from Carpenter's work. Carpenter's report of his visit to India in 1892,[2] his numerous articles on the *Upanishads,* his famous poem *Towards Democracy* (1883), inspired partly by his reading of *The Gita,* generated great interest in India. And Cousins explored deep into India and Indian philosophical thought, and wrote numerous works, which I thought should be examined critically and sympathetically by an able researcher. Mr. Dilip Chatterjee came to my help to take up the work which I would have liked to do myself. And he has done an excellent work digging up materials in Adyar Research Centre Library, Madras, Sri Aurobindo International Centre of Education, Pondicherry, Trivandrum Govt. Museum, Kerala, and in the files of old newspapers and periodicals, and has built a comprehensive image of Cousins and his works, beginning with his early Celtic Revival connections to the last days of his life in India. An expatriate Irishman who made India his home, and in his own poetic words -

---

1. See D.K. Barua, *Edward Carpenter* (1844-1929) *An Apostle of Freedom,* (1991) p. 138.
2. See Carpenter, *From Adam's Peak to Elephanta* (1892).

Who heard the sacrificial word
That frees the soul of man ;
He from golden stuff and silver thread
Through Celtic vision wrought
Vedantic thought ...

A magnetic personality, Cousins inspired many Indian writers and painters and presented them through appreciatory articles and reviews to the world at large. Sri Aurobindo, Sarojini Naidu and Rabindranath Tagore were among his friends. Mr. Chatterjee has done a commendable job by bringing all these materials to light and examining the Theosophical movement in the light of Cousins's work. I sincerely believe that this work will be considered a singal contribution to the growth of East-West understanding.

March, 9th, 1993 D.K. BARUA

ACKNOWLEDGEMENTS

This work could not have been undertaken if I did not get unfailing encouragement and supervision from my teacher Professor D.K. Barua of the Department of English, Burdwan University. I offer my gratitude to him for giving me the idea of working on Cousins.

I should also acknowledge the generosity of Burdwan University, specially the Research Board of the Department of English for giving me a University Fellowship for four years (1979-1982) to start my work on Cousins. Without this help my work could not have been undertaken.

I owe a special debt to Mrs. Radha Burnier, the President of the Headquarters of the Theosophical Society, Madras, who kindly permitted me to stay and work for some months in the Adyar Theosophical Society Library and Research Centre in 1980. I acknowledge the generous assistance of Dr. Pran Nath, the Librarian of Adyar Research Centre, in locating Cousins' works. I thank the Curator and the Librarian of the Trivandrum Government Museum who offered me his kind assistance when I worked there for some weeks. I also thank the Librarians of Madras University Library, the National Library, Calcutta, Visva-Bharati University Library, The Asiatic Society Library, Calcutta University Library and Burdwan University Library and Golpark R.K. Institute of Culture for extending all their facilities to me.

I am also indebted to the U.G.C., New Delhi, for granting me one years' Teacher Fellowship (From November 1986 to November 1987) in the Department of English, Burdwan University to complete writing my thesis.

I am grateful to Professor R.K. Das Gupta, former Director of National Library, Calcutta and one of the examiners of my thesis for his valuable comments and suggestions. I am thankful also to

Dr. (Mrs.) Ketaki Kushari Dyson of Oxford for her encouragement and assistance in my research work.

To Prof. Nilratan Mukherjee, my colleagues of Bangabasi group of Colleges and Rabindrabharati University I owe special thanks for inspiring me to publish this work. And finally, I should thank my wife Suprova and my brother Dipu for their uncomplaining acceptance of all the difficulties during this long period of my research work.

Calcutta - 400078 DILIP KUMAR CHATTERJEE

CONTENTS

INTRODUCTORY

James Henry Cousins, an Irish writer and a theosophist, was a younger participant in the Irish Literary Revival of which Yeats and A.E. were the leading members. His association with AE amounted almost to a discipleship and he followed all AE's interests including theosophy and social reform. In Dublin he was known as a journalist, a social reformer, a poet and a playwright. In all his literary and cultural activities he got active support from his wife Margaret Cousins. Together they devoted themselves to the Women Suffrage Movement in Ireland. They were the founders of the Irish Women's Franchise League. Herself a theosophist and feminist, Mrs. Annie Besant, knew Cousins and his wife Margaret well enough. She appreciated their activities and elected Cousins as her 'presidential agent' in Ireland in 1908.

Under her patronage Cousins and his wife came to India in November 1915. They settled down in Madras as active workers of the Theosophical Society. Mrs. Besant appointed Cousins sub-editor in her nationalist theosophical Indian Journal, *The New India*, published from Madras. Since then till his death in 1956 he lived in India and held various public positions. He made India his spiritual home and wrote poetry, drama, criticism and philosophical essays of considerable interest. Cousins' works, however, did not receive much critical attention.

Cousins' arrival in India synchronised with a new phase of Indian Nationalist Movement. This was the period when there was a kind of national resurgence in the literary and cultural fields, with Rabindranath Tagore, Sri Aurobindo and Sarojini Naidu as the outstanding writers with whom Cousins interacted. His close friendship and interaction with these Indian nationalists and poets provide us a perfect example of the East-West or to be more precise, the Indo-Irish interaction during the early decades of the twentieth century.

Considering that very little is known of this writer, my work tends to be bio-critical in nature and I endeavour to place the achievements of Cousins as a poet, playwright, critic and aesthetician in the light of the impact of the Theosophical Movement in India and the West.

I have tried to look at his life and work from the religious and historical perspectives of the late nineteenth century when a search for non-Christian faiths and wisdom-religion of India was manifest through various phenomena like the study of Comparative Religion, Spiritualism, Psychical research and the Theosophical Movement ; Cousins's life and works are all off-shoots of this milieu.

As Cousins derived his inspiration chiefly from two sources : The Theosophical Movement and the Irish Literary Revival, I have made two separate chapters ; one is devoted to the study of the fundamental tenets of theosophy and the other is to study the impact of Madam Blavatsky on some writers of the Irish Literary Revival particularly on A.E. and Cousins. Cousins' poetry and plays written in Ireland and India show his absorption of this dual heritage.

His literary criticism and aesthetical writings are not exempted from this attitude. Cousins' aesthetics grows out of years of viewing art and life in theosophical terms. He inherited the attitudes of the German Idealistic thinkers and Romantic Aestheticians and combined them with his theosophical philosophy. What he sought was to bring the creative intuition of the East and the critical intelligence of the West into a synthesis. He has significantly called his book on aesthetics, *A Study in Synthesis* (1934). Philosophically his interest in Indian thought or the ancient wisdom religion reflected his inner concern for a unitive experience where the human being would regain his wholeness.

He contributed immensely to India's social, cultural and educational developments ; in fact to almost every facet of the Indian awakening. His contributions to the development of Indian art and culture deserve to be remembered. He was one of the pioneers who sought to found an Indian academy of art. He also opened the first Indian Art Gallery, Sri Chitralayam, at Trivandrum in September 1935. His pioneering attempt to consolidate the cultural and spiritual unity of India is relevant even today.

Cousins' works *The New Ways in English Literature* (1917) and *The Renaissance in India* (1918) gave the impetus to Aurobindo to write his *The Renaissance in India* (1920) and *The Future Poetry* (1953). Cousins' book on Shelley, *Work Promethean : Interpretation and Application of Shelley's Poetry* (1933) is the first extensive study of Shelley from the Indian point of view and I think Aurobindo's interpretation of Shelley, was inspired by Cousins' book on Shelley. There are common grounds between Cousins and Aurobindo in their views on the trends of development in literature of the late nineteenth and early twentieth century.* This fundamental similarity between Cousins and Aurobindo has not received sufficient attention from Aurobindo scholars and critics because of the fact that Cousins' name disappeared from the literary horizon. When the personality disappeared from the scene his works disappeared from public notice and most of the Indian critics fail to assess Cousins' contribution as a literary critic.

He encouraged young Indian poets by writing Introduction or Foreword to their works. It was Cousins who first wrote of Harindranath Chattopadhyay in his book *Modern English Poetry* (1921). He wrote a 'Foreword' to Harindranath's first poetical collection *The Feast of Youth* (1918). So he did to F.A. Khabardar's *The Silken Tassel* (1918) and Rami Reddi's *Voice of the Reed* (1924). Similarly he inspired young painters by giving them expert reviews of their paintings and holding exhibition of their works at various places in India and abroad. The Bengal School of Painters specially owed him a debt for bringing them to a national as well as international attention. His sympathetic study of the painters of the Bengal School, young and old, appeared in two chapters of *The Renaissance in India.* It may be mentioned that he was the first western critic to study the paintings of Asit Halder and Promode Kumar Chatterjee.

His interaction with Tagore was equally fruitful. Tagore commended Cousins' views on education and Indian Culture and he

---

* See my article on this subject 'Cousins and Sri Aurobindo : A study in Literary Influence' in *The Journal of South-Asian Literature,* Vol. 24, No. I, Michigan State University, Asian Study Centre, U.S.A.

sent his aesthetic and philosophical work, *The Creative Unity*, to Cousins for review. Cousins wrote a perceptive criticism of Tagore's idea of nationalism in a long review article and helped to clear the fog of controversy and misunderstanding that cast a shadow over Tagore's commitment to nationalism.* It may be mentioned in this connection that when the suitability of 'Jana Gana Mana' as a national anthem was questioned Cousins justified this song as worthy to be the national anthem of India.

His remarks on Gandhiji's assassination were also an index of his deep involvement in the past and future of India. Like Tagore and Gandhi Cousins believed that the Unity of humanity must be recognised as the essential base of its struggle. He believed that India has a role to play in the resurgence of human civilization in our time not simply by overthrowing the yoke of the British but by deepening the impulse towards spiritual growth all over the world. He wanted to play the humble role of an interpreter and a link-man between the East and the West and to bring to light the new ideas of spiritual transformation that have been cultivated in India and abroad by various writers of his time. Cousins' life and work are a concrete embodiment of East-West understanding and their interdependence in efforts to create a new world of values based on spirituality and nationalism.

In fact, it is a pity that Cousins' life and work are so little known to the present day Indians. I hope that my work would be a humble attempt to fill in this gap in information.

See my article 'Cousins, Aurobindo and Tagore : A Perspective on their National Commitment' where I made a comprehensive study of this issue. I presented this paper in the International, Conference, 'Literature and Nationalism' organised by the Dept. of English, Rabindra Bharati University, Calcutta in September 1985. This Will be Shortly published in the forthcoming issue of the departmental Journal.

CHAPTER - I

J.H. COUSINS, A BIOGRAPHICAL BACKGROUND : FROM ULSTER TO ADYAR (1873 - 1956)

James H. Cousins (1873 - 1956), an Irish poet and thinker, an Orientalist, a powerful journalist, an educationalist, and art critic of eminence, was a younger participant in the Irish Revivalist Movement of which Yeats and AE were the leading members. He was a close associate of AE. His association with AE amounted to a discipleship and he shared his interest in Theosophy, the Irish dramatic and literary revival as well as his various ventures in social reforms. Both had an Ulster Protestant upbringing and a life-long interest in Oriental Philosophy and mysticism. Cousins considered AE a father figure in the Irish Literary Revival. He started his poetic career under the direct influence of AE. Some of his plays were produced in the early days of the dramatic movement in Ireland but were not much appreciated by Yeats who dismissed Cousins as one of 'AE's Canaries'.[1]

Cousins also received some unintended prominence when James Joyce made some derogatory comments on him as a publishing company chose to publish Cousins and rejected Joyce. The verse satire was of course directed primarily against the Maunsel Publishing Company of Dublin and was called "Gas from a Burner" (1912). Joyce wrote:

I printed mystical books in dozens
I printed the table-book of Cousins
Though (asking your pardon) as for the verse

---

1. This phrase was first used by George Moore in his memoirs. *Vale* (p. 169) ; see also Summerfield: *That Myriad Minded Man: A Biography of G.W. Russell - AE.* (Bucks, England : Colin Smythe, 1975), p. 115.

T'would give you a heartburn on your arse[2]

Here the reference is to Cousins' book called *Etain the Beloved and Other Poems*, published by Maunsel in 1912. Though Joyce dismissed Cousins' work as mere 'table-book' (an ornamental book, for a drawing-room table) and accused the Maunsel Publishing Company as a purveyor of mystical trash, yet one could not but acknowledge the contribution of this publisher to the Irish Literary Movement during the earlier phase.

Cousins like his mentor AE was committed to 'intellectual radicalism' of the period. John Wilson Foster in a recent article[3] has pointed out that his 'intellectual radicalism' was fundamental to most of the advanced Irish Revivalists. Foster says that 'the most graphic and succint evidence' of this particular trait of the Irish Revivalists, he found in the "the joint autobiography of James Cousins, the Ulster poet and his wife the Roscommon champion of Women's right, Margaret Cousins". Commenting further on James Cousins and his wife, Foster gives a list of their activities:

> The Cousins were involved in astrology, Theosophy and Psychism, in vegetarianism, agricultural co-operative, mythology, Gaelic language revival, dramatic revival, the Suffragette movement, Poetry, anti-imperialist agitation, Physical regeneration, anti-vivisectionism.[4]

Foster says that when one writes about "the supporters of this plurality of interests" and "the veritable nest of heterodoxies" in Dublin in the first decade of the twentieth century, "the same name (Cousins) drop again and again". This shows that James Cousins, though a minor writer, was quite well known in the intellectual circles of Dublin at that time.

Cousins was born at Belfast in Ulster in 1873. His mother was Irish and Welsh by ancestry, while his father was a descendant of Huguenot refugees and of English Elizabethan settlers in Ulster. Thus Cousins inherited the qualities of Celtic imagination from his

---

2. *The Penguin Book of Irish Verse* Ed. Brendan Kennelly (England, 1970), p. 321.
3. "The Interpreters" : A Handbook to AE and the Irish Revival, *ARIEL*, Vol. 11, No. 3, July, 1980, p. 69.
4. *Ibid.*

mother and the practical Anglo-Saxon ability of organization through his father.

His early life was full of vicissitudes; his education was "finished" at twelve. The so called National School of Belfast where he studied was not a nationalist institution and in fact was an instrument for denationalising its pupils. So Cousins continued his self-education in night schools, learning Scientific subjects and shorthand in which he specially attained very high proficiency. From 1889 to 1891 Cousins became a correspondence-clerk in Belfast Coal Importers' Office and from 1891 to 1894 he was employed as Private Secretary to Sir Daniel Dixon, the Lord Mayor of the city of Belfast. During this time Cousins acquired the skill of a "Verbatim reporter" and edited a shorthand monthly magazine, *The Irish Phonographic Bulletin.*[5] Though he trained himself to be a journalist he did not like the usual ways of the professional Journalists and their shallow outlook on things political. He says in his autobiography:

> Something in me revolted from the drinking that was general on the Press, and the easy way in which a man could transfer his allegiance from one political organ to its opponent. I decided not to be a professional journalist (p. 30).

However, it was at this period of his employment as Private Secretary to the Lord Mayor that Cousins discovered his ability to write verse. He continued writing and developed his gift rapidly, so that he brought out his first book of Poems *Ben Madhigan and Other Poems* in 1894. 'Ben Madhigan' is the Irish name for the 'Cave hill' which dominated the scene to the North West of Belfast, Cousins' native city. Here the young romantic poet presents a vivid portrait of his birth place. His next book *The Legend of the Blemished King* was published in 1897. The book was written as a result of his association with the Belfast Branch of the Gaelic League of which he was a member. The Gaelic League was founded in 1893 by an Irish Protestant Scholar Sir Douglas Hyde, with the object of reviving an interest in Gaelic Literature and, eventually, making Irish the national language of Ireland. Under the impetus of

---

5. *We Two Together* (Madras; Ganesh & Co. 1950), subsequent references to 'Autobiography' mean this work.

the Gaelic League Cousins read ancient Irish myths and legends and learnt Gaelic language and paraphrased some poems from the Gaelic as his fellow poets of the Irish Revival did. These books had more enthusiasm than art and Cousins has rightly dismissed them for their 'Juvenility of craft and content.' But they show his growing interest in the Celtic myths and lores which was fundamental to most of the Irish Revivalists of this time.

In fact, the main development of his poetic career began in the late nineties. Something inside was disturbing the growing poet. His sensitive and reflective mind became dissatisfied with the religious exclusiveness of his upbringing. The exasperating frustrations of life through poverty and restriction of opportunity made him rebellious. He found that the Church only offered the humiliation of charity and 'the hope of a hereafter over there'.[6] Like most of the late nineteenth century poets, Cousins was temporarily led to an intellectual agnosticism and scientific determinism which was fanned by his voracious reading of the six-penny reprints of the Rationalist Press. Huxley and Darwin became his secret scriptures. But he was essentially a man of religious temperament and found in AE's *Homeward : Songs by the Way* (1894), an affirmation he sought for. He took the book almost as a guiding star in life. He records his reaction to AE's poems in his autobiography:

> I read the little book (*Homeward : Songs by the Way*) through-in an interval and went on fire with the realization that immortal poetry had been given to Ireland. Our own attempts at verse were as nothing beside this voice...that uttered the most profound ideas and experiences in exquisite verse (p. 33).

Henry Summerfield in his biography of AE, *That Myriad Minded Man* (1975), observes that to some of AE's contemporaries *Homeward* brought a revelation of a new world. It is this revelation of a new world that lured Cousins to Dublin. Summerfield says: "In 1897...James Cousins, a naive idealistic young Ulster protestant, for whom the poems in *Homeward* were the most important thing in life, moved from Belfast to Dublin".[7] Fortunately Cousins

6. *We Two Together* (1950), p. 31.
7. p. 108.

succeeded in securing a job in Dublin, he was appointed an accounts clerk in a Coal Shipping Office.

He met AE for the first time on one Sunday morning at his salon at Rathmines and found that AE's interest were mainly in Theosophy and mysticism but what struck Cousins was AE's ability to reconcile his mystic vision with his pragmatic approach to social reforms. Cousins' contact with AE became more frequent and spiritually intimate; throughout the long sixteen years (1897-1913) of his stay in Dublin he belonged to an intimate circle of AE receiving new ideas and inspirations to write poetry.

It was under AE's direction that Cousins first studied Theosophical literature and books on mystical experience and in the beginning of the 20th century he found an entry into the literary world of Dublin with his three books of poems - *The Voice of One*, *The Quest* and *The Awakening* all carrying their mystical titles and the influence of AE.

Like most of the Anglo-Irish writers of the early 1900s, Cousins participated in the Irish dramatic movement, he was a close associate with the Fay brothers, Frank and William Fay,[8] who were as enthusiastic as Yeats, AE, Martyn and Lady Gregory, in building up a national theatre in Ireland. The Irish National Dramatic Company started by the Fays which afterwards became known as the Irish National Theatre Society, with Yeats as President and AE as Vice-President, and produced two one-act plays of Cousins in 1902. These were *The Sleep of the King* and *The Racing Lug*, one is a romantic verse play based on Celtic myth and was written in the tradition of Yeats' early plays and the other was more realistic in tone, written in prose, dealing with the tragedy of a sea-faring life which later became the subject of Synge's masterpiece *The Riders to the Sea* (1905). Amongst Cousins' other plays of this period we have reference to another play from the Bill of the Queen's Theatre which is entitled *Sold*. This was however dismissed by Yeats as trash, as by now Yeats began to dislike Cousins' plays. Yeats' adverse criticism brought about a temporary eclipse of Cousins' dramatic career in Dublin. Later in India he wrote two more plays:

---

8. For further information about the Fay brothers see James W. Fannery : 'The Fays and the Early Abbey Theatre' in *W.B. Yeats and the Idea of a Theatre* (Yale University Press, 1976), pp. 187-189.

one of them which deserves to be mentioned was *The King's Wife* (1919), a poetic drama based on the life of Queen Mira, the greatest Hindu singer of mystical and devotional songs, popularly known as Mirabai.

In Dublin Cousins was not only known as a journalist, poet and playwright but a competent teacher as well. After eight years as a clerk in Dublin, Cousins joined a High School in the post of an assistant master. He specialised in Physical Geography and Geology and became a demonstrator in 1912 at a Summer course for teachers run by Professor Herbertson of Oxford and Grenville Cole of the Royal College of Science of Ireland. For some time he worked for a diploma in Education in Trinity College, Dublin, but did not complete it.

During this period from 1905 to 1913, Cousins was also engaged in a variety of cultural and social activities. One of these significant activities is the involvement of the Cousins family in the women's Suffrage Movement in Ireland. With Francis Sheehy Skeffington, one of the most public-spirited men of Ireland of this time, who was later killed in the Easter Rebellion in 1916, the Cousins founded the Irish Women's Franchise League in 1908. They also brought out a weekly paper called *The Irish Citizen* devoting to the feminist cause. Mrs. Cousins was the Treasurer of the Irish Women's Franchise League and James Cousins was the Editor of the Journal *The Irish Citizen*.

The aim of the Irish Women's Franchise League was to obtain the Parliamentary Vote for the Women of Ireland on the same terms as men then had it. The League decided to co-operate where possible with the Suffrage societies of Great Britain and other countries, especially with the militant Suffrage organisations. From 1908 to 1914 the Cousins were fully involved with all the activities of the Franchise League. They organised a reception in Dublin in 1909 of the great English Feminist Christabel Pankhurst, the founder of the Womens Social and Political union in England, and took her in an organisational tour to various parts of Ireland, Mrs. Cousins was one of the six women from Dublin who attended the Parliament of Women organized in Caxton Hall, Westminster, on November 18, 1910 and demonstrated before the House of Commons along with 400 other delegates.

It may be relevant to note in this connection that the Cousins took feminism in a different spirit from those of their English counterparts. Everywhere they explained that the Irish Women's Franchise League was not absolutely 'identical in its militant methods with the English Suffragettes'. Mrs. Cousins said, "we were not attacking shop windows, emphasizing their non-violent approach.[9] In fact their feminism did not bring up all kinds of questions about the relation between the sexes. Nor was it pursued as an opposition to every aspect of patriarchal hegemony, political and cultural. As in India so in Ireland the Cousins intended to combine their Suffragette activities with the spirit of nationalism and social reforms. For which they were supported by social reformers, and political activists and literary men alike. Cousins' "Suffrage Sonnets" written during 1908-1910 reflected this involvement. His poem "To one in Prison" was written when Margaret Cousins was imprisoned in Holloway Jail, London, from November 23 to December 23, 1910 for her participation in the Women Suffrage Movement.

Besides the Suffragette activities, Cousins was closely associated with the co-operative movement in Ireland. In 1894 Sir Horace Plunkett founded the famous Irish Agricultural Organisation Society to promote the development of several kinds of co-operative Institutions especially the creameries and the Credit Banks. Plunkett appealed to the Irishmen's sense of patriotism. Both AE and Cousins responded to his call and their first task was to tour the congested districts in the West of Ireland addressing meetings and persuading the poor to organise Co-operative Banks.

This was a period when the writers of the Irish Literary Revival were working for a national resurgence of their country. Cousins' poem called "Ireland in Autumn" (1894) reflected this note of resurgence in sensitive terms:

> That Hand which bevels down the shortening day
> Is one with that which quickens leaf and wing
> So promise of resurgence in decay
> Thou hast, and in thine autumn, germs of spring.[10]

---

9. *We Two Together*, p. 185.
10. *Collected Poems* (1894-1940) (Kalakshetra, Madras, India, 1940), p. 11.

This 'Promise of resurgence' was the main content of the most eminent Theosophist Annie Besant's speech, "Theosophy and Ireland" which she gave in Dublin in 1902. This was the time that Cousins first met Annie Besant who had turned from her Fabian Socialism to Theosophy. Her speech made a great impact on Cousins. What Mrs. Besant wanted to emphasize in her lecture was that Ireland would ultimately emerge as the spiritual mentor of Europe, as India had long ago been to Asia. Cousins records his reaction to Annie Besant's speech in the following terms. He says: "I learned from her lecture that Theosophy was a much bigger matter than what I had derived from small manuals and so was Ireland".[11] He also says that it was Besant's speech which turned his "wishful thinking" into a conviction. This meeting with Annie Besant was so inspiring for Cousins that he was led to read Besant's theosophical booklet called *Esoteric Christianity* and got a deeper view of the realities behind dogma. He wrote in his autobiography: "I had worked my way through materialism, rationalism, blind faith and blind negation. In Theosophical writings I saw glimmers of light."[12] Cousins who found this 'light' first in AE's theosophical discourses became more convinced of it after Besant's lecture and reading her books. In 1908 he joined the Theosophical Society. His date of membership is dated, London, May 16, 1908. It was from this year that Mrs. Besant elected Cousins as her "Presidential agent" for propagating theosophy in Ireland.[13]

From 1980 to 1913 Cousins & his wife Margaret studied critically and experimentally the phenomenon of spiritualism which was not only a vogue in the Theosophical circle but amongst the educated men and women of the time as well. During this period the Cousins came under the widening influence of Prof. William Barrett and through him they were introduced to Psychical research. A branch of the Society for psychical research was established in Dublin during this period which followed the principles of the parent Society of London, founded in 1882 by Myers and Sidgwick. In connection with this branch a research group of intelligent, informed and highly placed men and women was formed. Cousins

11. *We Two Together*, p. 95.
12. *Ibid.*, p. 110.
13. Nethercott: *The Last Four Lives of Annie Besant* (Chicago: Chicago University Press, 1963), p. 133.

was a member of this Society of Dublin and he often discussed clairvoyance, telepathy and the spiritual interpretation of Celtic myths and folklores. In his book, *The Wisdom of the West* (1912) Cousins published a set of his lectures on Celtic myths. These lectures were given in the Psychical Research Society, The Theosophical Society, The Hermetic Society and in the Gaelic League. Here Cousins' interpretation of Celtic myths is tempered by his new knowledge of the occult Science and Eastern mystical lores which he must have derived from various books on comparative religion and Madam Blavatsky's magnum opus *The Secret Doctrine* and *Isis Unveiled. The Wisdom of the West* was published by London Theosophical Publishing House and was favourably reviewed by James Stephens in *The Irish Review* (April, 1912).[14]

Cousins' Eastern studies had induced in him a strong desire to go to India, and with this in view the left Ireland in 1913 to take up temporary preparatory work in Liverpool for going to India. A farewell meeting for him and his wife was held in Dublin Theatre. It was attended by intellectuals of all classes. Padraic Column, a contemporary poet and Cousins' friend, who came to his farewell meeting, wrote about the significance of the Cousins' association: "Walking the streets after the farewell I felt there was a deprivation in the forthcoming departure (of the Cousins) — there would be less goodwill in our midst".[15] This sense of being an instrument of goodwill among friends was also realized by James Joyce who after his stay with the Cousins in Dublin in 1913 appreciated their hospitality.[16] In this farewell meeting an address 'in illuminated book form' and a purse were presented to James and Margaret Cousins which indicated their popularity among intellectual circles of Dublin at that time.

But the outbreak of the World War I completely upset Cousins' plans for India. He and his wife came to Liverpool in England and settled down to work for various causes and social

---

14. Patricia Mcfate: *The Writings of James Stephens* (1978), p. 24.
15. Quoted by Alan Danson in his book, *J.H. and M. Cousins : A Bio-Bibliographical Survey*, England, 1967, p. 12. This mimeographed copy is available in Adyar Theosophical Society Library, Madras, India.
16. See Richard Ellman : *James Joyce* (1954), p. 177.

reforms. It was at this time that AE wrote to Cousins (on Oct. 15, 1913): "You are well out of Dublin these times. It is the most undrained swamp of humanity I ever heard of."[17] And again two years later on May 3, 1915, AE wrote to Cousins, "I hope you are getting on well in the land of the Saxons". Most probably AE knew Cousins' social and cultural activities in Liverpool.

During their stay at Liverpool Cousins and his wife participated in the food reform movement; his wife was elected as the President of the Liverpool Vegetarian Society. Cousins' essay called "The Philosophic Basis of Food Reform" seems to embody this spirit of the time. During this period the centre of the Cousins' religious, social and cultural activities was the Theosophical Lodge of Liverpool.

From Liverpool Cousins and his wife went to Sheffield to pay their homage to the English Socialist poet and thinker Edward Carpenter who was widely reputed in the Theosophical circle. They met Carpenter first in his Millthorpe house at Sheffield in 1913 and again in 1914. The Cousins were signatories in the congratulatory address to Carpenter on his Seventieth birth day in 1914 which was signed by the most eminent writers of the world. Carpenter who was interested in the Irish Revival, discussed with Cousins the poetry of AE and Yeats. He also talked to the Cousins about vegetarianism and the feminist movement of which he was one of the exponents. What interested Cousins was Carpenter's knowledge and appreciation of Indian Philosophy. Carpenter told him how he got a copy of the *Bhagawad Gita* from an Indian fellow student at Cambridge in 1883. This illuminating encounter with Carpenter at Millthorpe led Cousins later to write a short biographical sketch of Carpenter and an appreciative study of his vision of democracy in his book, *New Ways in English Literature* published in 1917. It was also through Cousins that Shri Aurobindo came to know of Carpenter's works.

Carpenter's interest in Indian thought and synthetic philosophy made a great impact on Cousins. He learned from Carpenter about his visit to South India in June 1890 and his varied

---

17. *Letters From AE*, ed. Alan Denson (London & New York, 1961) Letters No. 2, pp. 88-89.

experiences of seeing Indian life and culture. In fact, Carpenter stayed at Adyar, the Headquarters of the Theosophical Society, though he never belonged to their circle. Carpenter's book on India, *From Adam's Peak to Elephanta* (1892) increased Cousins' interest in India.

Cousins' interest in India became more intense after his meeting with Carpenter and fortunately in 1915 the 'call' came from Mrs. Annie Besant who wanted the help of the Cousins in her cultural and educational activities in India.

Cousins with his wife Margaret landed in India in November 1915 which was a critical period in Indian history, a period of turmoil in social and political scene. It was this year which witnessed two significant events bringing about a new tide in Indian politics. One was Mahatma Gandhi's return to India after his glorious struggle against the apartheid system in South Africa and the other was the Home Rule Agitation started by Annie Besant and Bal Gangadhar Tilak. Mrs. Besant (1847-1933) who in connection with her Theosophical Society had been doing immense service in the regeneration of India, formed the Home Rule League in India in 1916. With her Irish connection she wanted to follow the pattern of the Irish Home Rule Movement. One of the fundamental aims of Annie Besant's Home Rule League was to rehabilitate the self-respect of the Indians. It was to this effect that she founded The Hindu College in Benaras in 1898 which later became the nucleus of Benaras Hindu University. The series of Lectures she gave in Madras in 1913 were published with the significant title *Wake Up India*. These lectures stirred the minds of most of the educated Indians and they were inspired by Annie Besant's indomitable spirit of selfless dedication to the cause of Indian nationalism. What she stressed in most of her lectures was that Indians must awake and claim their respectful place as a nation in the British Commonwealth.

She knew that this awakening of the people could be achieved only by the expansion of education. The Theosophical Educational Trust which she formed in 1913 was intended to initiate reforms in education and to rid the people of thoughtless imitation of English habits and customs. In fact Annie Besant's work was a challenge to the Christian Missionaries who were busy in undermining the ancient Hindu ideals through their system of education. Annie Besant wanted to restore the element of self-consciousness in the culture and civilization of the East which was fast losing its hold on Indian minds due to their imitation of an alien culture. She wanted the Indians to develop their education in consonance with the high tradition of Eastern culture on the one hand and to absorb the best features of Western Culture on the other. With this view in mind she promoted national schools and colleges for boys and girls all over the country. She urged for independent educational Boards to be set up by the communities to further the growth of genuine national Institutions and helped build a net work of national education.

This concern of Annie Besant's Theosophical Society for education brought about a new dimension to the Theosophical Movement in India in the first two decades of the twentieth century. Annie Besant who was instrumental in bringing the Cousins to India, knew that India needed persons like them for her social, religious, educational and cultural regeneration. She had been watching over the Cousins with a considerable interest since 1908, the year she elected James Cousins as her "Presidential agent for Ireland" to propagate Theosophy. She was quite impressed by James Cousins' journalistic and literary pursuits and his wife Margaret's keen interest in the Suffragette Movement. Herself a feminist, Annie Besant appreciated the Cousins' close association with the English feminists Pankhurst and Mrs. Pethick Lawrence. She was therefore quite hopeful that the Cousins could be of great help in intensifying her theosophical, and educational activities in India.

James Cousins was first appointed a literary sub-editor in Annie Besant's nationalist and theosophical Journal *The New India* first published from Madras in 1915. He was expected to improve the literary side of the journal by virtue of his valuable experiences in journalism in Ireland.

Cousins' interest in Indian thought and Oriental culture was not new. In fact a strong feeling was generated by the Celtic Revivalists that spiritually Ireland belonged to the East. Hence the Irish nationalists developed a bond of spiritual kinship with their Indian counterparts. In 1915 when Cousins came to India, he found the atmosphere of the country alive with the nascent upsurge of the nationalist movement. The Celtic nationalist movement with its eagerness to establish contact with the spiritual movement of the East had already planted in Cousins the seeds of a common interest. They blossomed now in a life of committed service in contact with the Indian nationalists. In fact the situation of India and Ireland as oppressed nations in the British empire, brought a bond of sympathy among the nationalists of both the countries. So Cousins had no difficulty in identifying himself with the Indian awakening of the post (First) World War years.

Cousins believed that the only service essential to the cause of India's regeneration was to encourage and rehabilitate Indian ideals in the field of art, literature and education. While working as a sub-editor in *The New India* he came to know of a group in Bengal who were working to strengthen a new school of national art known as the Indian Society of Oriental Art, of which Abanindranath was the chief exponent.

The Indian Society of Oriental Art which was formed in 1907 in Calcutta, was an association of Indian and European gentlemen, the object of which was the cultivation among its members and the promotion among the public of a knowledge of all branches of ancient and modern Oriental art. It was under the auspices of this Society that the work of Abanindranath, Gogonendranath and some other new Bengali artists had been exhibited annually to the public, Cousins first learnt about this movement through the *Modern Review*, a widely circulated Journal published from Calcutta, which became an important organ of Indian renaissance. Cousins first saw the paintings of the Bengali artists in the pages of the *Modern Review* and was inspired to write his first short article on art criticism, "Art of the East" (1915).[18]

Commending the works of the Bengali artists Cousins pointed out that he saw some similarity in the activities of the Indian artists to express the soul of India with his fellow Irish poets and painters of his time. He, therefore, could speak to them with the experience of Irish experiments. He warned that while the Indian artists may enrich themselves by the imitation of the West, they should not do

---

18. This article was later developed into two significant chapters, 'The Bengal Painters: First Impression-1916' and 'The Bengal Painters: Second Impression-1918' in Cousins' *The Renaissance in India* (1918).

so at the expense of their own "native spirituality-their natural expression of quiet tones and simple themes" which according to Cousins, were the quintessence of the Indian temperament. "The Art of the East" (1915) was appreciated by most of the leading figures of the Indian Society of Oriental Art. O.C. Ganguly a powerful Bengali artist and art critic of the time, sent Cousins his book on Indian art and sculpture called *South Indian Bronzes* for review in *The New India* along with a letter of appreciation of Cousins' comments on the works of the Bengali artists.

Cousins, who was aware of his own limitation, knew that his knowledge of the works of the new Bengali artists was confined to colour productions in *The Modern Review* once a month. What he needed most at that time, was a direct knowledge of these works. This opportunity came to him when he received a letter, dated 6 January, 1916, from Sir John Woodroffe, President of the Indian Society of Oriental Art, inviting him to Calcutta to see the 8th Annual Exhibition of the Society and write about it in the *New India* and other papers. Cousins took this letter immediately to Mrs. Besant who encouraged him to come to Bengal.

Cousins had a great admiration for Bengal for her cultural heritage and political sensitivity. In fact, Bengal during this period played a crucial role in the awakening of India and own an important position in Indian history. Cousins knew that it was Calcutta, the chief city of Bengal, which was chosen as the centre of cultural and reform activities by another Irish expatriate, Margaret Noble (1867-1911), later known as sister Nivedita, who came to India in 1898 and lived till her death in 1911. There was another attraction for Cousins in Bengal, which was to see the world famous Bengali Poet Rabindranath Tagore who won the Noble Prize in 1913. It was this experience of visiting Bengal and developing direct contact with the leading figures of its cultural and revivalistic activities that led Cousins to write his inspiring book *The Renaissance in India* in 1918. The book was significantly dedicated to the art leaders of Bengal:

> Dedicated to Sir John Woodroffe, Lady Woodroffe,
> Abanindranath Tagore, Gogonendranath Tagore,
> Ordhendra Coomar Ganguly and N. Blount through
> Whom I found the way towards the secret of India.

This book expressed Cousins' deeper understanding of the spiritual, mental and emotional forces which were at work in terms of art and literature.

In order to gain a direct knowledge and perception of the Oriental Art Movement Cousins came to Bengal in 1916. He reached Calcutta on 14 January, and was received by Sir John Woodroffe, a judge of the High Court, whose interest in the Hindu tantra was widely known. Cousins was introduced to the Tagores and other leading figures of Art movement in Bengal. Here his primary duty was to report to the *New India* on the exhibition of paintings organized by the Indian Society of Oriental Art. Cousins was so impressed with the paintings and the manifestation of their national spirit in their art that he requested the organizers that the exhibition should be shown also in Madras. Cousins records in his autobiography that he could easily persuade them as: "I guaranteed (in faith) that the paintings would be dealt with expertly and be given a dignified and intelligent display in a suitable place under the most distinguished auspices."[19] He succeeded in organizing the first exhibition of modern Indian paintings in South India under the distinguished patronage of Mrs. Besant, C.P. Ramaswamy Aiyar, B.P. Wadia, the Chief Sub-editor of the *New India*, and the Governor of Madras, Lord Pentland. Pentland however was suspicious of the activities of the Cousins and he "put Ireland and *New India*" together and connected Cousins with some articles on aspects of nationality published in *New India* with the by-line "An Irish Home Ruler". In fact, during this period Cousins wrote his essay, "The Policy of the open door"[20] (1919) criticising the British Government for their Industrial Policy and aggressive commercial outlook.

The exhibition of paintings of Indian Society of Oriental Art of Bengal made a stir in the cultural life of Madras. It got wide newspaper publicity and was appreciated by the art lovers of South India. Cousins thus succeeded in giving this local movement an all India outlook by means of his extraordinary skill of organization

---

19. *We Two Together*, p. 266.
20. See Chapter 7, *Footsteps of Freedom* (Essay), (Madras: Ganesh & Co., 1919), p. 73.

and publicity and they came to be widely known as one of the most sympathetic critics of Indian art and culture.[21]

Within this short period as a Sub-editor of *New India* Cousins earned a wide recognition from all corners of India. Mrs. Besant found in Cousins a valuable aide who could combine the roles of a travelling companion, secretary and an intellectual assistant. She was well aware of Cousins' brilliant journalistic career. Yet for some reasons she could not confirm his job as a sub-editor in the *New India*, Cousins had to switch over from journalism to education.

In 1916 he was appointed a Lecturer in English in the Theosophical College at Madanapalle, a small town in South India, which became later a popular tourists resort as the birth place of a "World Teacher" J. Krishnamurti. The College was opened in 1915 and was in its initial stage when Cousins was appointed. Mrs. Margaret Cousins was appointed an assistant teacher of English in the adjoining national high school from which the college had been developed. The national school and the college were run by Besant's Theosophical Trust. Mrs. Besant knew that James Cousins had some years of experience in school teaching in Ireland in national high schools and she was confident that he and his wife both could devote themselves to her theosophical and nationalistic education which she was trying to develop in the whole of the country.

In the beginning, Cousins and his wife were not very happy with the educational atmosphere of Madanapalle College. They sought for something more humane and creative than teaching rudimentary English to the Indian boys and girls whose interest in education was limited to preparing some notes to pass the examination. Cousins' duties also included those normally performed by a Bursar both for the college and for the adjoining national high school where Mrs. Cousins was working. The creative and most dynamic personalities like the Cousins could not be

21. It is very surprising that Partha Mitter's *Much Maligned Monsters* (1977), an authentic study of the history of European reactions to Indian art, does not mention Cousins. It may be noted that Cousins in collaboration with Stella Kramrisch wrote a book *The Arts and Crafts of Kerala* (1948), reprint 1970.

complacent with their teaching assignment. Both of them were preparing their future plans. They now concentrated on education for Indian women and children. Mrs. Cousins inviting ladies to her college residence started teaching the Indian women some kind of vocational education. In one of her visits to Burma she learnt how to make articles of daily use from cane. She now demonstrated this new art to the members of the Society and helped them making baskets for fruits and flowers, plates for carrying offerings to the temples. What she and her husband intended to cultivate in the Indian women was not only vocational interest but the development of love, mutual respect and confidence in their minds. Mrs. Cousins with her agreeable manners and her pleasing personality endeared all including the Brahmin ladies who in the beginning showed some reservations. This was the nucleus which was later developed into a large and important Indian Women Association in July, 1917. Mrs. Besant was the President of this first All India Women's Organization and Mrs. Cousins remained the Secretary from its inception to the thirties of this Century (1917-1937). This centre was transferred later to Adyar, Madras, in 1922.

The year 1917 became the most significant date in the life of the Cousins in India. In this year Mrs. Besant with her two collaborators in the Home Rule Agitation, George Arundale and B.P. Wadia, were interned. Rabindranath Tagore protested against this internment in an 'Open Letter' in the journal *Bengalee* dated 17 June in 1917. Mrs. Cousins who was a born rebel, took this opportunity and organized a protest meeting in Madras. She spoke for the first time before the public on a political platform condemning the British. Mrs. Besant was released in September 6, 1917. Mrs. Cousins and her husband who were planning to do something for the emancipation of Indian women, wrote in this year a letter to Prof. D.K. Karve of Poone University to launch a movement claiming votes for Indian women. Mrs. Cousins applied her previous experience in political activities in Ireland and organized a deputation of Indian women on the subject of their right to vote before Mr. R.S. Montagu, the Secretary of State for India. She drafted the address; while drafting the address Mrs. Cousins said: "I had to balance up my perhaps exaggerated fighting spirit with the Indian quietism when I came to the point of drafting the first request for votes of Indian women".[22] On December 18,

22. We Two Together, p. 311

1917 the deputation was led by Sarojini Naidu who was the official leader and the unofficial ones were Annie Besant and Margaret Cousins. Mrs. Manomohan Kaur has rightly pointed out that Margaret Cousins and her husband were the progenitors of the idea of vote for women in 1917. Both of them were ardent suffragettes and champions of women's cause all over the world.[23]

Towards the end of this year the Cousins accompanied Mrs. Besant to Calcutta to attend the 33rd session of Indian National Congress held on December 26, 1917. Mrs. Besant was elected president in this meeting. With Besant the Cousins also attended the first official meeting of the Board of National Education which was held in Calcutta in December 22. Here Mrs. Besant proposed to set up a National University at Adyar. Tagore was elected Chancellor of the University. This was Cousins' second visit to Bengal, and he wanted to make a good use of it. He and his wife were invited to the Tagore Mansion at Jorasanko where they saw the performance of Tagore's Symbolic play, *The Post office*. They also visited the Bose Institute of Sir J.C. Bose and was honoured by the hospitality of his accomplished wife Lady Abala Bose. Mrs. Bose later became very close to Margaret Cousins in connection with her franchise and female education activities in India. Mrs. Cousins presents an interesting study of her friendship and association with three of India's most notable women, Ramabai Ranade, Sarojini Naidu and Abala Bose, in her book *The Awakening of Asian Womenhood* (1922).[24]

Though Cousins was promoted to the post of the principal of the Madanapalle College in 1918 he managed to keep his interest in

---

23. 'Civil Disobedience Movement 1930-1935', *Women in India's Freedom Struggle* (New Delhi, 1985), pp. 183-186.
24. For an appreciative review of this book see *The Calcutta Review*, Vol. 8, 1923. The reviewer recognizing Mrs. Cousins' leading role in the awakening of Indian and Asian womanhood observes: "Mrs. Cousins has a wonderful capacity of understanding, the Asiatic and especially the Indian Psychology. She has so completely become one of ourselves that she is fully entitled to speak for our women. Like that other noble soul Nivedita, She has correctly interpreted the yearning, of the Asiatic Women's heart...She sees the woman of Asia coming to the fullness of her stature as the equal partner of man. Mrs. Cousins has tried to show us something of this new spirit awakening into consciousness."

creative writings. During his three years' stay in India he wrote two significant books entitled *New Ways in English Literature* (1917) and *The Renaissance in India* (1918) which brought Cousins to the attention of some Indian intellectuals including Sri Aurobindo. Sri Aurobindo recognized Cousins as one of the powerful literary critics of modern English poetry and appreciated Cousins' knowledge and depth of scholarship of Indian art and culture. In his review of the first number of *Shama'a*, a nationalist and literary journal published from Madras under the Editorship of Mrinalini Chatterjee (1920), Sri Aurobindo admires Cousins' article, "Symbol and metaphor in Art". Sri Aurobindo calls it "quite the best thing in thought and style in the number."[25]

New Ways in English Literature and *The Renaissance in India* and a number of poems that Cousins wrote during this period, show his growing awareness of a new perspective in literature and thought. As he took interest in National Education he started travelling extensively during this period with the objective of spreading throughout India the significance of National Education. During this year Cousins was also invited to speak on the role and significance of drama in the national awakening by the Amateur Dramatic Association of Bangalore. This lecture was later developed into a book and was published as *The Plays of Brahma* in 1921. Speaking about the use of drama in a period of national awakening Cousins here reminds us of the ideals of the Irish Dramatic Revival, the fundamental aim of which was the discovery of the national identity of the Irish. Cousins advised Indian Playwrights to write drama as an "Instrument of realisation of the national activity of India" as the Irish writers did in their country in the early years of this century.

Through all these activities Cousins became widely known and he came to be friendly with many important Indian personalities such as Gandhi, J.C. Bose and Tagore. It may be mentioned in this connection that Cousins gave a talk on these three great Indians in a literary and Cultural Club in Washington, U.S.A. in 1930. He called his lecture "the Saint, the Scientist and the Seer of modern India". Rabindranath Tagore was called a 'Seer' by Cousins and Tagore showed a considerable interest in the activities of the

---

25. See *Views and Reviews* (Pondicherry, India, 1941), p. 94.

Cousins. He visited the Cousins at Madanapalle in February 1919. He was accompanied by C.F. Andrews, Tagore's co-worker in Santiniketan. Tagore was quite impressed by the educational atmosphere of Madanapalle College and School and called this place the "Santiniketan of the South".

As a sequal to Tagore's visit Cousins went to Santiniketan in April 30, 1919. He discussed with Tagore various aspects of Education, exchanging ideas on its implementation with the teachers and staff of Santiniketan. Tagore appreciated Cousins' ideas on education and Indian Culture and he sent his aesthetic and Philosophical work, *The Creative Unity*, to Cousins for review in 1922, and the review appeared in the *Modern Review* in July, 1922 (p. 66).

From Santiniketan Cousins set out for Japan for one year on a Professorship in the Keijuku University of Tokyo. Unlike other professionals Cousins was not interested in career building, he was more interested in being involved in meaningful causes. Though he had to devote a lot of time to the preparation of lectures on modern English poetry at the University, he utilized his time in Japan in making innumerable acquaintances, significant of them were his friendship with the Japanese thinker, writer and artists like Okakura, Nuguchi, Taikwan, Tami Koume and Paul Richard, the French mystic and the pacifist staying in Japan during that time. While in Japan Cousins reacted strongly to the growing Japanese habit of imitation at the expense of their Eastern spirituality. He had an interview with Tami Koumi, the modern Japanese Painter, whom he criticized for imitating the western painters. In his article called "Modern Movements in Japanese Painting" published in an Indian Journal *Shama'a* (Oct. 1922, p. 18) Cousins observes: "Modern Japanese art had not merely run away from Classical Japan, but had bolted head down into the arms of the bad angel of western art". That Cousins is always in the quest of a positive national outlook in art, is evident in his criticism of the Japanese painters. He found their attitude a negative one:

> I wanted a positive thought to give me a sense of reality. It came to me with increasing certainty that Japan's way of escape from artistic insultarity-her way of recovery of her primal Inspiration, *Lay in a return to India - not necessarily the*

India of the map, the region of spiritual realisation and enthusiasm".

(Emphasis mine)

It is interesting to notice here Cousins' thought that India could be the source of a spiritual revival in the whole world. He wanted the Japanese to look back to their ancient heritage derived from India wherefrom they got their religion. His remarks on English Literature of the 1890s was equally influenced by this thinking. He thought that the influence of Indian thought could give a fresh direction to western literature. Cousins had an interview with another Japanese artist, Taikwan, who admitted the weakness of modern Japanese Painting and promised Cousins, "One day I shall express the pure negotiation of spirit with spirit" - an ideal which was always insisted upon by Cousins in his criticism of art and literature.

During his 'Japanese year' Cousins became more involved in the Pan-Asian revivalist movement which was then developing in Japan as a reaction against industrialisation and the spread of materialistic outlook of the west. This was known as the Pan-Asian Spiritual Revial, a movement aimed at the rediscovery of the spiritual unity of Asia.[26] While he was in India Cousins had already found that a considerable number of Asian thinkers took as their primary task the revitalization of ancient ideals of all Asian countries most of which were British Colonies. Some of these Asian thinkers who sought to infuse new spirit into the minds of their people and help reawakening their glorious heritage, were Okakura, Tagore, Gandhiji, Sree Aurobindo and Noguchi. All these leaders of Asia strove in their various ways to redeem their cultural and artistic heritage and spread its message throughout the world. This created a new desire of East-West understanding and a large number of writers and thinkers were influenced by this reawakening of the spiritual heritage of the East. During the first two decades of this age there came a large group of writers, scholars, mystics and social thinkers to India some of whom had

26. Stephen Hay : *Asian Ideal in East and West* (Combridge, Mass Harvard University Press, 1970), p. 313. See also Eugen Hoeflich : 'Pan-Asia' in *The New Orient* (U.S.A.), Vol. II, No. I, May-June, 1924, p. 21.

contributed to the growth of the culture of the East. Amongst these who deserve to be mentioned in connection with the spiritual reawakening of Asia, were Margaret Noble (Sister Nivedita), Annie Besant, Paul Richard and his wife who later became the Mother in Sree Aurobindo's Pondicherry Ashram. Among others are Count Keyserling, C.F. Andrews and James Cousins who, as Stephen Hay pointed out, contributed a lot to the *elan* of the Asian revivalist activities.[27]

Cousins as one of these ardent revivalists of Pan-Asian spiritual revival, travelled far and wide in the East, and was seized with the conviction that there existed a single unity which might be called Oriental, Eastern or Asian. Like most of this group he shared "a stronger belief in the East." He shared with Okakura, Tagore and Sri Aurobindo, the Asian's pride to the uniqueness of their heritage and he corroborated this in most of his writings. In the book called *The Cultural Unity of Asia* (1922), for instance, he called "India, the mother of Asian culture". He said that "in Asia all roads lead to India - or, rather, all roads lead from India" (p.133). He was sure that the unitive vision of Indian culture and philosophy could provide an answer to the world of problems. Cousins' faith was accentuated by his theosophical belief and his study of the works of contemporary Western pacifist and writers like AE, Edward Carpenter, Paul Richard, Romain Rolland, all of whom affirmed that Asia could be the saviour of the war-ridden West. Roman Rolland, the French pacifist, novelist and a friend of India, wrote to Tagore in April 1919 to ask his help in bringing "the intelligence of Asia into closer touch with European thinkers".[28] He said "My dream will be that one day we may see the union of these two hemispheres of the Spirit."[29] What Rolland intended was to re-establish the union of the East and the West and their healthy development. Tagore who wanted to foster this harmony between the cultures of the East and West wrote : "Now has come the age of Co-ordination and Co-operation...So we must prepare the grand field for the Co-ordination of the Culture of the world...We must base our own structure on a synthesis of all the different cultures we

---

27. Stephen Hay, p. 314.
28. Stephen Hay, p. 128.
29. Ibid.

have".[30] Cousins became more friendly to Tagore and his friendship with the great poet, inspired him to build up his philosophy of Synthesis. He dedicated his book *The Cultural Unity of Asia* to Tagore, the founder of Visva Bharati, who in Asia became one of the chief exponents of East-West understanding. Cousins found an affinity with Tagore's educational ideas and he said in his autobiography: "I realised from the copy of his (Tagore's) *Creative Unity* that the poet sent to me, *how close our minds were in the philosophy and technique of what we believed to be true education*".[31] (Emphasis mine)

At the end of his one year Professorship in Japan in March 1920 Cousins returned to India and rejoined his duties in the Madanapalle College as the principal on April 18 and continued in his office until summer 1922. Returning to India Cousins was much disturbed to find the country in the midst of Gandhiji's Non-co-operation Movement which started in 1921.

Non-co-operation Movement upset Cousins because it undermined the educational activities. Annie Besant also came out openly against Gandhiji on this Non-co-operation issue and so did Tagore. Tagore asked bitterly : "Our students are bringing their offering of sacrifices to what ? Not to a fuller education but to non-education."[32]

What Cousins and Tagore wanted is to bring a resurgence of India through educational ideas and they were not thinking simply in terms of nationality but as human beings or human society as a whole. They wanted to humanise and spiritualise education against the corruption of modern civilization. They wanted to bring aesthetic education into the centre of educational activities. Cousins said in one of his essays : "We should humanise and spiritualise eudcation by bringing doll-dressing and boat making into it; in short by making play as important a branch of education

30. See Stephen Hay, p. 108.
31. Stephen Hay, p. 344.
32. See S. Sinha, *Social Thinking of Rabindranath Tagore* (1962), Chap. 'The ideas of Swaraj', p. 125.

as the dreary grind called work."[33] We find similar ideas in Tagore's philosophy of Education.

Tagore in his visit to Madanapalle appreciated Cousins' efforts in introducing art and crafts in the School and College curriculum. Both Tagore and Cousins were keenly aware of the importance of the aesthetic side of education. Cousins' essay "The Relationship of Culture and Training" sought to establish this connection. Here Cousins said : "Departmentalism, water-tight compartment can have no place in an educational system. We need an all round, balanced development of the nature of the student. There should be nothing in school study that cannot be related with life; and there should be nothing in school training that is not balanced by and directed towards culture".[34]

Cousins realised that education is the only answer to regional rivalry and linguistic conflicts. Thus he travelled throughout the country to co-ordinate cultural and educational activities which were going in different region and linguistic areas of India. He wanted to bring them in touch with each other; and to give them a national consciousness in their pursuit was Cousins' aim. In the *Shama'a* (October 1923, pp. 64-65) under the Column 'Notes and Comments' the following preliminary notice was issued by Cousins to achieve this purpose :

> During several tours which I have made through most of the linguistic areas of India, I have come in contact with various wellmarked movements in creative literature and the fine arts. These movements, separated both by distance and language, are working independently and in ignorance of one another. Yet, while rightly developing along the lines of local traditions, they are obviously simultaneous diverse expressions of a cultural awakening which is not merely provincial but Indian; and as such, they will fail of their highest accomplishment if not brought into sympathetic relationship with one another.

---

33. Chap. 'The Relationship of Culture and Training', *Footsteps of Freedom,* p. 134.
34. Chap. 'The Relationship of Culture and Training', *Footsteps of Freedom,* p. 134.

It is quite evident in this notice that Cousins sowed the seeds of ideas which have grown now into Institutes like Sahitya Akademy and Sangeet Natak Akademy. Though a foreigner Cousins had this insight and our nation has to be grateful to him. In his travel around the country he came across numerous artists, poets, painters whom Cousins gave publicity and patronage and brought them to national prominence. Among them were people like A.F. Khabardar, G.K. Chettur, Kanu Desai, Asit Haldar and Promode Kr. Chatterjee. Incidentally it may be mentioned that Cousins was the first person to see the significance of Tagore's 'Jana gana mana' which he insisted that Tagore should translate into English. Tagore obliged him at Madanapalle and the translated song was called "The Morning Song of India."[35]

To Cousins this poem expresses the quintessence of India, a land where races, cultures and religions have merged to form a grand unity. He also mentioned that this poem is a witness of the spirit of racial tolerance, co-operation and collaboration which is the basis of Indian Culture. So for Cousins it was not simply a national anthem of India but an international song of universal brotherhood of man. It may further be mentioned that when a controversy started about the fitness of the song as a national anthem Cousins came forward to defend it in newspapers emphasizing the poet's philosophy of human unity embedded in the poem. Cousins records in his autobiography that this was sung in his School as a prayer song since 1934. He said : "Every working morning 'Jana Gana' is sung by hundred of young people in our big hall (at Madanapalle). We want to extend its purifying influence by sending copies of it to other schools and colleges in India and by making it known abroad".

Cousins visited Tagore for the second time in 1921 and he and his wife stayed at Santiniketan about a fortnight. They stayed very close to Tagore's Cottage Uttarayan and were invited to discuss with him the poet's scheme of creating an International University. It was in this year (December, 1921) that the Visva-Bharati was founded. Cousins was also closely associated with the *Visva-Bharati Quarterly;* the first issue of this journal carried Cousins' essay called

---

35. Cited in Prabodh Chandra Sen : *Bharater Jatiya Sangeet (Indian National Anthem)* (1949).

"Poetry and World Problems" which is a splendid defence of Shelley.[36] He contributed to this organ of Tagore's cultural and artistic vision, several articles since its inception. The Cousins' autobiography, *We Two Together*, records vividly their days spent with Tagore. What remained an unforgettable experience with Cousins was Tagore's discussion of philosophy, art and literature with him in the fall of the dusk and in the peaceful serenity of Santiniketan. It seems that Tagore's Philosophy of harmony which was the central focus of these informal discussions, influenced Cousins in formulating his philosophy of synthesis or 'Samadarsana'.

It was with this idea of achieving unity through synthesis of religion, art and education that Cousins, with the assistance of Annie Besant, J. Krishnamurti. B.P. Wadia, developed Brahmavidya Ashram or the School of Universal Study at Adyar. The Brahmavidya Ashram or the School of Universal Study was a winter school where the session started from October to March.[37] Here the courses were given in comparative religions, philosophy, art and literature and the principal object was to develop an awareness of a comman basis of World's Cultural Unity. The *Shama'a* October issue (p. 54) observes on the activities of Cousins in the School :

> From the programme of work that is carried on now, and under the care and guidance of J.H. Cousins, an Irish poet and art critic of eminence, who is the Director of Studies, the Ashrama bids fair to blossom into another International University, a meeting ground of the World's religions, cultures and civilisations - another step towards the fulfilment of its idea - the Brotherhood of Man irrespective of Caste, Colour, Creed or Sex.

The note assumed that the other Institution was Santiniketan of Tagore. As a Director of Studies of this School Cousins gave lectures on mysticism, religion, philosophy, art and education. These lectures from 1922 to 1928 were later collected and published under the title *A Study in Synthesis* in 1934. The first session of the School was held on October 1922 and continued upto March 1923.

---

36. See *Visva-Bharati Quarterly*, Vol. I, No. 1, April 1923, pp. 54-68.
37. See *We Two Together*, p. 393.

Similar Annual sessions followed, of which the last ended in March 1928.

In 1929 while Cousins was busy developing the school of Universal study at Adyar he was invited by the University of Calcutta to give two post-graduate lectures on art and cultures.[38] Sir Ashutosh, the Vice-Chancellor of the Calcutta University, presided over these lectures. Appreciating Cousins' lectures on Indian art and his activity in the cause of its revival, Sir Ashutosh promised Cousins that the University would bring out these lectures in a book form but the plan fell through after his death.[39]

During this visit to Calcutta Cousins gave lectures in the Bengal Theosophical Lodge, in Buddhist Vihar, and in the Indian Society of Oriental Art. This last lecture was published under the title "The Future of Indian Art" in the *Rupam* (No. 17, January 1924, pp. 43-48) the journal of the Society, which was highly appreciated by most of the art critics of the time. The *Rupam* also published an interview with Cousins where he was praised for his knowledge of Indian art and culture and his strenuous efforts in propagating the ideals of Oriental Art throughout India and abroad. The Interviewer introduced his observation with the following comment : "He is one of the pillars of support which it has been the good fortune of the Neo-Bengal School to secure from this good friend of India.[40]

Cousins' love for Indian art led him to found in 1924 the Jagan Mohan Chitrasala in Mysore City. It was the first permanent and compendious Gallery of modern Indian paintings in South India. In the inauguration ceremony his Highness The Maharaja of Mysore, Sri Krishnaraja Woodiyar G.C. S.I. welcomed Cousins to the State as a friend of Indian art and culture.

---

38. See *Calcutta Review*, Column 'Ourselves', Vol. 8, 1923, p. 134. "The Senate has, on the recommendation of the Council of Post-Graduate Teaching in Arts, invited Mr. J.H. Cousins, D. Litt. to deliver two lectures on 'The Cultural Aspects of the Renaissance in India" Dr. Cousins has a genuine insight into the mysteries of Indian Culture which is a sealed book to many an acute non-Indian."
39. *We Two Together*, p. 399.
40. *Rupam* (Calcutta) No. 11, July, 1922, pp. 99-101.

He invited the Cousins to participate in the Dasara ceremony, the greatest festival of Mysore. Though they were foreigners they were specially Permitted by the king to see the festival from close quarters in its entirety as a result of which Cousins wrote an interesting study of the symbolical aspect of the festival which was published as a booklet, *The Dasara of Mysore* in 1925. The Dasara celebration at Mysore in King's palace in the autumn of 1924 gave the Cousins ten days of the utmost artistic and social joy. At the end of the festival the king requested Mrs. Cousins to give a piano-recital in his palace. Thus they became quite friendly with the king and his family. The king presented them a cheque for Rs. 1000/- in appreciation. This enabled Cousins to visit Europe and America in 1925. During this visit Cousins was not forgetful of his mission. He gave a number of lectures on Indian art and culture in some of the foremost cultural centres in Europe, Geneva, Paris, New York for example. He also gave Lantern Lectures on Modern Indian Paintings in Paris.

In this visit he met two theosophical painters, one was the Belgium Painter Jean Delville and the other was the Russian Artist and Sculptor Nicholas Roerich. Roerich was an Orientalist. His Paintings on Indian themes were permeated with a keen interest in Indian life and culture. Cousins was so inspired to see the paintings of Delville and Roerich that he wrote a book on their paintings called *The Great Theosophist Painters Jean Delville and Nicholas Roerich* (1926).

Cousins' work as an exponent of Indian art and culture in America and Europe was not confined to public Lectures. He gave poetry recitation often selecting poems of Tagore and some other Indo-Anglian poets, of whom he wrote in *New Ways in English Literature, The Renaissance in India, Modern English Poetry* and *Samadarsana*. Here he also met people in Symposia and held exhibitions of Indian Paintings. What he aimed at through these activities was to unfold the spirit of Indian art and culture to the Western audience. In 1930 he was appointed a Visiting Lecturer in Modern English Poetry in a College of New York.

When he returned to India after this second visit to Europe and America he found political tensions in the country gathering momentum. When communal riots and wrangles broke out all over the country, Cousins and his wife devoted themselves to social work to help improving the situations.

It is impossible to understand Cousins without understanding the activities of his wife Margaret Cousins who supplemented him in all activities. So we may note some of Mrs. Cousins' activities as an inspiring leader of Women's organization in India. She was a friend of Sarojini Naidu, and Kamala Devi Chattopadhyay whom she called 'my spiritual daughter'. During the general election of 1936 Mrs. Cousins actively canvassed for Kamala Devi Chattopadhyay; she also organised an All India Women's Conference on Educational Reform which was held in Poone in 1927. She organised the first All Asian Women's Conference held in Lahore from 19 to 25 January 1931. She thereby enlarged the scope of her feminist activities to the whole of Asia. She raised funds and laboured hard to make the feminist activities a success. She was also closely associated with the publication of the *Stri Dharma*, the main organ of the Indian Women's Association. She became its Editor for about a year (1935-1936).[41] On December 10, 1932 Mrs. Cousins was arrested on the charge of making speech against the Government Ordinances supporting Freedom of speech and movements. Her speech from the dock is well worth remembering :

> The fact that I am on trial on this court today is no accident. It is the result of sixteen-years of intimate living and working with my Indian sisters and brothers. In moving freely with them in attempting to do constructive work, I and my husband learned how exploitation and injustice through foreign rule is crushing them down. I was a co-worker for Home-Rule for years with Annie Besant, and took part in the agitation connected with her internment in this cause. I also shared in formulating the commonwealth of India Bill. Government repression of organised Congress opinion, the largest

41. For further information about Mrs. Cousins and this Journal see R.K. Sharma: *Nationalism, Social Reform and Indian Women* (New Delhi, 1981), p. 85 and 191. Another critic who assessed the contribution of Mrs. Cousins to the feminist movement of India is P. Asthana. See her book, *Women's Movement in India* (Vikas, New Delhi, 1974), pp. 67-68.

representative opinion in India, has become ever more severe since then. I watched it in 1930-31. I reported what I had seen, in New York and Geneva during my visits there in the past 18 months. In those Centres of international opinion I laid bare the dual game Britain is playing : its pretence of making a constitution to give India freedom but its determination to hold tight to everything essential to India's self-Government. I showed that its demand for unity and Social reforms as necessary to Swaraj were conditions such as no country had ever complied with. I prove that instead of freedom, Government by Ordinances was designed to break, if possible, the spirit, ruin the health and cripple the resources of all the people of India who are determined to win the political freedom they want. Representative associations of eighteen countries have deputed me to tell the people here that they "sympathise with them, and that they denounce the rule of violence now imposed on India". as the New York protest meeting expressed it. Now that I return, I find that the ordinances have been made into law for three years. This is a challenge to every believer in free speech, free political assembly, free press, free picketing, free peaceful self-expression, I adhere to everything I said in public. I reiterate that the Ordinance Bill and Ordinance Law should be made inoperative by every one ignoring them by non-violent defiance. Evidently the Government think me a valuable ally of the Congress when they priced my freedom by bail at thirty thousand rupees. If it is their intention to strike me dumb for a year, are we to deduce that their new constitution is going to be so unsatisfactory that I must be locked up for all that time to prevent any criticism of it ? If this is British justice and democracy, then I am proud to stand here in support of free speech and Indian national freedom, and I am ashamed that English idealism has fallen to the present depths of oppression and suppression.[42]

Meanwhile Cousins continued his duties as a principal of Madanapalle Theosophical College. His wife was released in October 21, 1933 from Vellore Jail, Madras. Mrs. Besant died in

42. *We Two Together*, pp. 582-83 also cited by Kaur.

this year. Cousins organised a commemoration committee to publish Annie Besant Commemoration Volume which came out eventually in 1947. In 1934 Cousins was appointed a part-time Art-Adviser to the Government of Travancore which he held upto 1948, for two years the appointment was a full time. He helped to establish Sri Chitralayam(Art Gallery) of the State of Tranvancore which was opened to the public at Trivandrum by His Highness, Maharaja of Travancore in 1935. The Maharaja in appreciation of Cousins' activities in the revival of Indian art and culture conferred on him the title the 'Veera Srinkhala' and presented him with the Pandit's Shawl. At the opening of this Art Gallery on 25 September 1935, His Highness the Maharaja made special reference to Cousins' Contribution in the following terms :

> It is a matter for congratulation that Dr. Cousins, the well known exponent of art and literature, has succeeded in assembling this collection of paintings from many places designed to include the various schools of modern paintings in India. He has spared neither effort nor time in equipping this gallery with rare and representative specimens of pictures and colour prints, and I gladly take this opportunity of expressing my deep appreciation of the valuable service rendered by him and I hope that this institution will continue to receive his fostering care.[43]

In 1935 another pleasing experience appeared to Cousins; this was O.C. Ganguly's reception given to him at his home in Calcutta. Here Cousins met most of the leading painters of Bengal. In the reception Abanindranath Tagore offered the vote of thanks for Cousins' glorious activities in the cause of the revival of the Indian art. Towards the end of this year (December 1934) the South India Teachers Association conferred on Cousins the title 'Kulapati' for his distinctive services to Indian art and education. In 1936 Cousins left Madanapalle and came to Adyar to become the Director of Akademy of Arts later known as Kalakshetra. During this year Cousins was also associated with the Temple Entry Movement in South India. As he was a spokesman of human and religious unity he became directly involved in this movement with Dr. Ramaswami

43. *Speeches and Messages of the Highness, the Maharaja of Travancore* (Compiled and Ed. G.P. Sekhor, Trivandrum, 1938) p. 107.

Aiyar and His Highness the Maharaja of Travancore. When the Maharaja opened all the temples within the state to all classes of Hindu, irrespective of caste, it was Cousins who drafted the speech of Maharaja. Gandhiji visited Travancore to celebrate this Proclamation in January 13, 1936. In the following year Cousins was ceremonially admitted to Hindu Worship adopting a Hindu name Joyram. From April 25 to June 27 of this year Cousins accompanied the Maharaja in an educational visit to Java and Bali. This provided him with further insight into Eastern Art and Culture. In October of this year he was appointed Curator of the Government Museum, Trivandrum and the Sri Chitralayam on a salary of Rs. 700/- per month. He held the post for two years. In 1939, his health having been undermined by the climate, he continued in office only on a part time basis. In September 1941 the Annual Session of the All India Educational Conference was held. Cousins here addressed the delegates on "Art in Education". He also organised an exhibition of Modern Indian Paintings at this conference. In this year Tagore died; Cousins paid a tribute to the great Indian poet through a remarkable essay 'Tagore on Tagore'. This was contributed to the book *Gurudev Tagore : A Garland of Tributes to the Memory of Tagore*, published in 1946 and was edited by R. Narasimhan, Secretary of the Tagore Society of Madras. In December 1943 Cousins won the highest recognition of the Theosophical Society, George Arundale, the President of the Theosophical Society, Madras, India, conferred on Cousins the Subha Roy Medal of the Society for his lifelong pursuit in propagating the Theosophical ideals in the field of art, education and culture. In 1943 Mrs. Cousins fell seriously ill and she was taken to Nilgiri Hills for her recovery. She did not fully recover and after living almost as a cripple for ten years she died in March 1954 at Adyar. In 1944 Cousins gave George Stanley lecture in Madras University which was published under the title *The Aesthetical Necessities in Life* (1944). Cousins summarises the content and purpose of these lectures in the following terms :

> On the side of "aesthetical morality" I shall do no more than refer, as I have already done, to the ancient Indian teaching of the use of appropriate pictures as means for the development of desired virtue through which one may obtain individual release from the demands of the lower nature, and so become a better citizen. This is the gist of these lectures as it applies to

> art appreciation as an essential means for the encouragement of a new world order.[44]

Cousins also rendered an immense service to the cause of the revival of arts and crafts in Kerala. He collaborated with Mrs. Stella Kramrisch, the American Indologist and art critic, to publish an important book called *The Arts and Crafts of Kerala* in 1948. Mr. V. Vishwanathan, the Governor of Kerala while writing a 'foreword' to this book mentioned Cousins' contribution in this sphere. He said, "The Contribution of Dr. J.H. Cousins is an abiding testimony to his genius in the interpretation of an aspect of Kerala Art, the importance of which was not recognised before." Cousins' interest in the folk art and dance of South India led him to devote the last days of his life to the Kalakshetra, one of the Important Centres of Indian Art & Crafts, with Miss Rukmini Arundale. He became the Vice-President of this Centre of art in 1949 and remained in this position till his death in 1956.

As a summary of Cousins' activities in India we may conclude our assessment in the words of O.C. Ganguly :

> If three Englishmen - Hume, Wedderburn and Cotton awakened in Indians a thirst for political independence, three other radiant personages - Miss Margaret Noble (Niveditā), Sir John Woodroffe and James H. Cousins awakened our thirst for cultural and spiritual emancipation.[45]

---

44. Chap. 'The Influence of the Objective Arts on Life', p. 74.
45. *Sister Nivedita Birth Centenary Souvenir* (First Series) Calcutta, 1956, p. 33, ed. by Prof. Sankari Prasad Basu & S. Ghosh.

CHAPTER - II

THE THEOSOPHICAL MOVEMENT — HISTORICAL SETTING

In the earlier Chapter we have given a rapid survey of Cousins' life and activities from Ireland to India - from the place of his birth and the arena of his life's activities. But a person like Cousins is interesting for us, because he is a by-product of some representative historical, cultural and religious forces which originated in the later part of the 19th Century and created the climate of mind which has continued up to our times. Owing to conflicts between science and religion, social developments and ideological growth, religious thinkers since the mid-nineteenth Century have developed an interest in the study of other religions besides Christianity. Hence the emergence of what has come to be known as a study of Comparative Religion.

Frederick Denison Maurice's *Religions of the World and their relation to Christianity* (1847), his 'Boyle lectures', may be considered a representative by-product of the period. It was an outcome of his reaction to Carlyle's dogmatic comments on Muhammad and Islam in the lectures on *Heroes and Hero Worship* (1840). The Rev. Frederick Denison Maurice, the most respectable theologian of the Anglican Church, was a representative figure of the mid-nineteenth Century theological development. He emphasized on the positive features of all religions and that all religions played a historical part in the development of human consciousness - and observed that the world had never been without a witness of God. So all historical religions should be considered as a vehicle of the growth of human spirit or as Maurice himself put it, 'the spiritual nature and faculties of man' (pp. 246-247).

In the Chapter entitled 'Man's Relation to Divine Nature' (Part II, Lecture II p. 173) Maurice discusses sympathetically the Vedantin doctrine of Brahma and affirms :

> Such a view of the Divinity, and of the way in which man is related to Him, is found in different modifications among all those people who are members of what is called the Indo-Germanic Stock, and perhaps, in some who do not belong to it (p. 173).

Summarising the essence of different religious faiths, Eastern and Western, Maurice affirms, 'look at these religions, and you see in them all a witness of unity' (p. 174). Maurice frankly admits the Value of 'Hindooism', Buddhism and Muhammadanism in his 'Boyle lectures' and says :

> Our obligations to them are not slight if they have been sent to break down a low grovelling notion we had formed of our own position and work... we owe them the deepest gratitude if they have led us to ask ourselves whether there is any faith, and what kind of faith it is, *which must belong, not to race or nations, but to mankind* (. 245) (emphasis mine)

This comparative approach to world religion and the search for a universal religion beyond race or nation but of mankind, made Maurice's writings an important document of mid-nineteenth Century religious trends.

Mention should also be made of Maurice's pioneering effort in his Boyle lectures towards a Psychological and spiritual interpretation of myths and folklores. In a Chapter called 'A Reality in the Pagan Mythologies' Maurice argues that the myths and folklores should not be dismissed as 'Pagan' for they often express a 'cry for the Infinite beyond' - this anticipates later scholars of comparative religion and particularly Madam Blavatsky. Maurice's writings on comparative study of religion are undoubtedly responsible in creating an interest in Indian thought in the heart of the Anglican Church and India emerged as a centre of religious curiosity in mid-nineteenth Century. Buckle in his famous *History of Civilizations* (1857) chose India and Greece for special study because he said, 'our information respecting these countries is most extensive and has been more carefully arranged' (p. 147). Frederick Denison Maurice published a prose resume of the *Bhagwad Gita* in his study of *Ancient Philosophy* (1850). It is of interest to note that between 1885 to 1888 six translations of the *Bhagwad Gita* appeared in England alone not to mention several other publications in India, America and on the continent. We must not also forget the great service rendered by Emerson and other Transcendentalists in America - which created the background for the later development of the Theosophical Movement.[1]

No examination of the background of the Theosophical Movement can fail to take into account the importance of the Transcendentalist Movement in America. Transcendentalism, a philosophical and literary movement, flourished in New England from about 1830 to the early 1860s. This movement has generally been attributed to the influence of German thought transmitted by Wordsworth, Coleridge and Carlyle. Transcendentalism drew on European idealistic philosophy and the Romantic movement. This eclectic movement collected its ideas from different sources and Indian Philosophical thought provided principal support to all the leading figures Emerson, Thoreau and Alcott since its inception.

The movement represented a revolt against rationalism and also institutional religion. Thoreau wrote that he preferred to hear cow bells to Church bells on Sunday morning. Emerson propagated the theory of the 'Oversoul' and the unity of God, man and the universe which are quite similar to the concept of Brahma of the Vedanta. In his journal of 1868 Emerson recorded that in the history of intellect there was no more important fact than the Hindu theology. He saw Indian thought also as an antidote to the tide of materialism. Emerson often quoted Hindu Scriptures in his writings which reflected a number of things later to surface in Theosophy : eclecticism, antipathy to institutional religion and the interpretation of dogmas of Christianity in a new perspective, to name a few.

It was because of Emerson's efforts to create an interest in Indian thought that transcendentalist movement may be called a precursor of Theosophy. It was Emerson's discriminating eclecticism which administered the severest rebuke to the

---

1. I owe much of this background information to D.K. Barua's book, *Edward Carpenter : an apostle of Freedom* (1991) Burdwan University Press.

prevailing prejudice against Oriental religions and Philosophy and inaugurated an age favourable towards the reception of ideas from the Orient.

Spiritualism was part of a reaction that developed in America against the rigidities of Puritan Christianity. The movement sought to inculcate a spirit of independence from the tyranny of Calvin's God. It began with the idea of immortality of soul and the survival of sentient spirit after death. The cult of Spiritualism, in the sense of communication with the spirits of the dead, is supposed to have originated at Rochester, New York, with the mediumship of the Fox Sisters in 1847. The Fox Sisters sought to provide assurance of immortality through their communication with the spirit. From this bizzare beginning the movement spread rapidly to all parts of America and to England and France. In the fifties and sixties of the 19th Century the spiritualistic excitement was in full swing, with many extraordinary resources accredited to its exponents.

The introduction of Spiritualism in Great Britain is usually attributed to an American medium Mrs Haydon who came to England in 1852. A year later the British Spiritualist Church was established at Keighley, Yorkshire, and two years later the first British Spiritualist Newspaper *The Yorkshite Spiritual Telegraph* was published from the same town. The Spiritualism gradually spread and finally it engaged the attention of famous scientists like Michael Faraday and A.R. Wallace, Sir William Crooks and Prof. De Morgan. A.R. Wallace, the co-discoverer with Darwin of the Theory of Evolution, wrote a series of articles 'In Defence of Spiritualism' in *The Fortnightly Review* which were later published as a book in 1874. The same year Crooks published his *Researches in the Phenomena of Spiritualism* which he carried on with a famous medium, Florence Cooke. Unlike Darwin, who was rather prone to agnosticism, Wallace was a religious man, but not a professing Christian and later he gravitated to Theosophy.

Spiritualists proclaimed that they had been able to bridge the chasm between science and religion with empirical proof of life after death. They believed that they were making a contribution to empirical science by their séance experiments, and they appealed to what they believed were objective data.

In fact, Spiritualism depended on and gave expression to Western occultism. Occultism which glorifies 'unreason' against the tradition of the rationalist Enlightenment of the Eighteenth Century, expressed itself as a discovery of interest in the esoteric cults of the Cabalists, the Rosicrucians and the Alchemists. Occultism in the Western tradition was a source of inspiration for the leaders of Spiritualism. The level of participation in this movement is a significant fact in the history of the Western Religious thought in the nineteenth Century. What attracted most of its adherents was that Spiritualism sought to satisfy certain emotional needs in people who were deprived of any belief in personal immortality.

But in spite of so many adherents Spiritualism may be said to have been an amorphous movement with no solid philosophy of its own. The exposure of wide scale of fraud led many to leave the movement and is probably the major cause of its decline after about a decade. In addition, the association with unpopular causes such as free love proved embarrassing. Spiritualism did not develop any organizations beyond a few local and temporary associations. It also failed to respond to the higher cravings of the soul and hardly approached the nobility and beauty of that conception of Eternal life which has been developed by the mystic philosophy of the Orient.

Theosophical Society inherited this climate of opinion created by the Spiritualists. The forces that were generated and promoted by Spiritualism included anti-clericalism, anti-institutionalism, eclecticism, social liberalism, and belief in progress and individual effort.

In the seventies there was a desire to work toward a reconciliation between science and religion and it was hoped that Oriental thought would work as a catalyst in achieving this reconciliation because vitalistic science can be sustained by some ideas derived from Hindu religion. There was present also a hope that Oriental Philosophical ideas could be integrated into a grand religious synthesis.

The Theosophical movement of Madam Blavatsky aimed at transcending the cleavage between science and religion by a return to the concerns of an ancient wisdom tradition, long forgotten.

Theosophy meaning 'divine wisdom' signified a revival of ancient speculative systems, particularly those connected with a Neo-Platonic thought. The objects of her Theosophical Society were :

(1) to encourage each member of the society to study and develop his "inner Psychic Self";

(2) to oppose the materialism of science and every form of dogmatic theology, especially the Christian; - to make known "the facts about Oriental religious Philosophies, especially the pure esoteric teachings in the Vedas, and in the Philosophies of Buddha, Zoroaster and Conufucius";

(3) Chiefly to aid in "the institution of Brotherhood of Humanity, wherein all good and pure men will recognize each other as the equal effects (upon this planet) of one Uncreate, universal, Infinite, and Everlasting Cause."[2]

Belief in universal Brotherhood and the emphasis on the value of Oriental religions formed the Central tenet of the Theosophical society. Theosophical Society owed to Madam Blavatsky for her organising ability and her powerful literary studies. Madam Blavatsky's principal works were the *Isis Unveiled* and *The Secret Doctrine* and they constituted the basic texts for Theosophy. We are taking a detailed account of Blavatsky's works because most of the Theosophical Writers reflect her ideas, images and phrases.

Blavatsky's important work *Isis Unveiled* (1877) claims that religions of the world have all been derived from a single, primitive, source (II, 639), an ancient universal religion known to both Plato and the ancient Hindu sages (I, xi). Every religion is thus based on the one and the same truth (I, 444) : the "Secret doctrine" or wisdom, identical in every country. The work speaks of recognition of the Hermetic Philosophy or ancient universal wisdom region as "the only possible key to the Absolute in science and theology" (I, vii). The "secret doctrine" contains the "alpha and Omega of Universal Science" and is the keystone to ali knowledge both ancient and modern (I, 511). This 'Secret Doctrine' or 'ancient wisdom' of the esoteric tradition of religion was the base of all

2. Josephine Ransom : *A Short History of the Theosophical Society* (Madras, India, 1938), p. 105.

religions. The discovery of this wisdom is an answer to the religious conflict of the contemporary world. In the opening chapter of the *Isis Unveiled* the intention of Blavatsky's work is declared :

> We must show our false theologies in their naked deformity, and distinguish between divine religion and human dogmas. Our voice is raised for spiritual freedom, and our plea made for enfranchisement from all tyranny, whether of Science or Theology (p. 51).

Here Blavatsky wanted to attack the twin enemies of the period mechanical Science and dogmatic Theology - theosophy offers spiritual freedom from their rigidities.

The *Isis Unveiled* is divided into two volumes, the first entitled "Science" and the second "Theology". The first volume has chapters on Spiritualism, Modern Science, Psychic Phenomena, Mesmerism, the Kabbala, the knowledge and achievement of ancient peoples and psychic feats and wonders. The second volume contains a great deal of polemical material against Christianity, a discussion of Secret Societies, estoeric interpretation of Christianity and other religions; further it contains a treatment of the Kabbala and a comparison of Christianity with Hinduism and Buddhism.[3]

Beneath the diversity of topics treated, there is an underlying theme : the work is a treatise on the ancient wisdom religion. This theme explains the appeal of *Isis Unveiled* to its late nineteenth Century audience. Its readership has been composed to a large extent of educated persons to whom religion was important but who had been estranged from institutional religion. Their learning made them seek an answer to the challenge of science to religion and made them eager for insights from different religious tradition. The idea of wisdom - religion, a universal and ageless occult knowledge derived from a civilization in which there was a unity between science and religion, suggests a possible common ground and a way to integrate the insights of the various faiths into a grand synthesis. It may be mentioned that ideologically such a faith was more

---

3. For discussion of Blavatsky's texts in this section I owe to Campbell's *Ancient Wisdom Revived : A History of the Theosophical Movement* (University of California Press, U.S.A., 1980).

suitable to an age which was on the threshold of a politics of universal empire.

There are a number of important themes related to the major idea of an ancient Wisdom - religion. First the book presents an emanationist view of the world (I, 154, 285, 275).[4] This theory posits the physical devolution of man from "Higher and more Spiritual natures" (I, 295). There was first an involution : the descent of a "divine spark" into matter (I, 301). That spark is now climbing to its source (I, 301, 303, 319). This hermetic theory of evolution, movement upward to the source and return, embraces Darwinian ideas in a larger synthesis :

> all things had their Origin in spirit - evolution having originally begun from above and proceeded downward, instead of the reverse, as taught in Darwinian theory. In other words, there has been a gradual materialization of forms until a fixed ultimate of debasement is reached (I, 154). [5]

This is putting the idea of evolution on its head - evolution is a process of debasement of the spirit which had to be reversed. She propounds that the theosophical 'Ancient Wisdom' is built into a colossal scheme of world history, which makes out the human species to be much older than what Palaeontologist suppose even today.

Blavatsky's treatment of the evolutionary theory is as striking as her esoteric interpretation of the Bible. The term Christ, for instance, is used to mean the "Personal divinity indwelling in man" (II, 574). Much of the polemic against Christianity in the work assert that the Bible merely copies older works (II, 405, 408, 422, 428), that Jesus' teachings are not original (II, 45, 49, 51, Chap. 6), and that Christian practices and rites are identical to those of the ancients (II, 94). It states that there is one source of all religions and of science : "the yearning of the imprisoned human soul for intercourse with supernal spheres" (II, 639). The source of all religions and science - Blavatsky suggests, is a secret occult brotherhood that has conserved the wisdom tradition through the ages (I, 573). "The ancient 'Kabbala', the gnosis, or traditional

4. Campbell, p. 37.
5. Ibid.

Secret knowledge, was never without its representative in any age or country" (II, 38). These secret fraternities of adepts, Blavatsky thinks, hold the key to the understanding of miracles, psychic phenomena, and life after death and themselves possess remarkable occult powers (I, 406, 456-457, 500, 573, II, 106-107, 402-403, 590).[6]

Madam Blavatsky's *Isis Unveiled* despite its verbose and sometimes confused or unsystematic argument was considered to be an achievement or a 'milestone' in the history of Western Occultism. Here she gathered a number of central themes from the occult tradition - the idea of an ancient wisdom, an emanationist cosmology, the concept of Adepts, an esoteric interpretation of Christianity and discussed them in relation to current development in science and the new knowledge of non-Western faiths. Making use of contemporary Western Occult works and ideas, *Isis Unveiled*, reflected controversies of its time - particularly the implications of Darwinism and of Asian religions for the West and expressed a response that appealed to intelligent persons of the time interested in religion but alienated from its conventional Western forms. This work of Blavatsky is also important as first statement of ideas on the Occult - amplified in later Theosophical writings, particularly for its affirmation of an esoteric religious tradition. *Isis* gives occult themes a Western cast and is linked with current problems of Christianity.

Madam Blavatsky's second volume *'The Secret Doctrine* which is regarded as her masterpiece was published in 1888. It seems to be a recasting and amplification of *Isis Unveiled*. The book claims to be based on the "Stanzas of the Dyzan", a mysterious ancient religious text unknown to scholars. The first volume, entitled "Cosmogenesis" deals with the creation of the universe. The second volume "Anthropogenesis", concerns with the history of the earth and particularly the evolution of humanity through a succession of great "root races". *The Secret Doctrine*, in fact, seems to be compiled by Blavatsky from various nineteenth Century books on Occultism and comparative religion.

'The Secret Doctrine', Blavatsky claims, is the "Original element, out of which every mystery and dogma has grown,

---

6. Campbell, p. 38.

developed, and become materialized" (I, viii). As for content, *The Secret Doctrine* is based on three fundamental principles : (i) the existence of one absolute Reality, the infinite and eternal cause of all ; (ii) the periodicity of the universe : its appearance in cycles ; and (iii) the identity of "all souls with the Universal Oversoul : the pilgrimage for every soul spark through the cycle of Incarnation" (I, 14-17).

In *The Secret Doctrine* Blavatsky uses a number of Oriental ideas, the period in which the universe remains in its latent or resting state is called *Pralaya*, the state of the Absolute during Pralaya is called the 'Night of Brahma', when nothing is in existence, but every thing exists in an eternal present. Blavatsky says that "We have finished the descending arc and begun our return to Deity, both the globe and the human family on it. Exiles from God, prodigal sons in a far country, we have set out on *Our homeward Journey* (emphasis mine)".[7]

Volume two, "Anthropogenesis contains discussion on symbolism and of the relation of the 'Secret Doctrine' to science, but its principal concern is the history of the earth and particularly the evolution of the races up to the present. This story of cosmic and human evolution is the backdrop for the theme that explains the deep and abiding interest the book has held for occultists over the last century. A single quotation shall summarize the work. Speaking of the 'Secret Doctrine', Blavatsky writes : "It is the Spiritual evolution of the *Inner*, immortal man that forms the fundamental tenet in the Occult Sciences" (I, 634).[8]

The Secret Doctrine provides an answer to the religious strife of the age explaining man as a solitary cosmic pilgrim. Man has a two-fold nature. He is Monad or Spark of the Infinite Essence, and he evolves through a mind and a body. The challenge of human evolution is explained as the need for the higher part to attain a right relation to the lower. The work thus suggests the reason for individual suffering-estrangement of the two parts - but it also holds out the hope that individual effort can alleviate suffering. It pictures the fate of the individual as predetermined in important respects,

7. Kuhn A.B., *Theosophy : A Modern Revival of Ancient Wisdom* (New York, 1930), p. 209.
8. Campbell, p. 45.

but it leaves open a significant area for free and responsible action by which the individual can improve himself, by his karma and reincarnation, the twin concept framing the theosophical view of human destiny.

Blavatsky insists on the inner potentiality of man and claims that man needs no institutional religion, man can have direct religious experience. Endowed with divine powers and feeling in himself his inner God, each can feel that he is a Man-God, though an animal in his physical self. Blavatsky says that the legend of the "fallen angels" contains the key to the contradictions of human character. A grasp of this doctrine gives a clue to the question of the origin of evil and shows how man himself is the separator of the one into various contrasted aspects. The 'fallen angels' contains the key to the contradictions of human character. A grasp of this doctrine gives a clue to the question of the origin of evil and shows how man himself is the separator of the one into various contrasted aspects. The 'fallen angels' are actually humanity. The demons of pride, lust, rebellion, hatred had never had any existence before the appearance of physically embodied conscious man. Man has "contaminated the indwelling god in himself, by linking the pure spirit with the impure demon of matter (II, 274). She affirms that there was never an 'Original Sin' but only an abuse of physical intelligence, the psychic being guided by the animal, and both putting out the light of the Spiritual (II, 413). Fall of man is not seen as the consequence of an act of mortal man, but rather as the 'Fall of Spirit into generation' (I, 192). History begins with the descent to earth of the gods, who incarnate, themselves in mankind, and 'this is the Fall' (II, 483). She has also presented her concept of Avatar or Incarnation in this regard. 'Avatar' she says, is the fall of a God into generation (II, 484).

Blavatsky exploits the language of science and the myth of the Bible and thus seeks to answer spiritual questions in the language acceptable to contemporary men.

Madam Blavatsky exercised a great influence on some mystically oriented Western writers of the later half of the Nineteenth Century and the beginning of the present age. These imaginative writers were fascinated by the occult symbolism that Blavatsky employed in her writings. Their imaginations were stimulated by the mythologies of religion that had a universal base.

This could be understood by applying the 'Keys' of esoteric knowledge that unlocked the symbolism of gods and heroes. They thought that her system made religion vastly more interesting and more exotic. The impact of Madam Blavatsky's Theosophical writings upon literature has been widely acknowledged by several critics of the late nineteenth century - notably John. A. Lester in his *Journey Through Despair : 1881-1941 Transformation in British Literary Culture (1968)*. Marcea Eliade in his *The Occult and the Modern World* noted this *fin de Siécle* interest in the occult of some French Writers of this period. He says that even a sceptic like Anatole France declared in 1890 that "a certain knowledge of the occult sciences become necessary for the understanding of a great number of literary works of this period. Magic occupied a large place in the imaginations of our poets and novelists".[9] He has cited *La-Bas* (1891) by J.K. Huysmans as inspired by occult lores. Eliade also observes that during 1890s a number of English writers become involved in occult practices and eagerly sought to be initiated into secret hermetic societies. Among these writers and poets Eliade mentions W.B. Yeats, S.L. Mathers and Aliester Crowley. In the theosophical and occult lores most of these writers were looking for Pre-Judeo Christian and Pre-Classical (Pre Greek) elements i.e. Egyptian, Persian, Indian or Chinese Creative methods and spiritual values. They sought their aesthetic ideals in the most archaeic arts, in the 'Primordial' revelation of beauty.[10] In his effort to evaluate the process of civilization, D.H. Lawrence turned to theosophy and occult lores. His interest in theosophy was aroused by his reading of Blavatsky, Annie Besant and James Pryse. Pryse, the author of *The Apocalypse Unveiled*, provided Lawrence with a theosophical idea that beneath the Christian surface of the 'Book of Revelation' the symbols of Pagan mysteries lay concealed. Lawrence's *Apocalypse* (1931) is supposed to be based on the writings of Pryse and Blavatsky and reads almost like a theosophical tract.

These writers and poets found new sources of inspiration in Madam Blavatsky's treatment of myths and folklores which she considered as the reservoir of ancient Wisdom. They became

9. See Chap. 4 'Nineteenth Century French Writers and their Interest in the Occult' p. 51.
10. Ibid.

genuinely interested also in such theosophical themes as cycles, reincarnation, the succession of gods and the cult of eternal mother that underlies all ancient religions. Madam Blavatsky's writings provided them the hope in personal and cosmic *renovitio.*[11] Her writings also became a source of inspiration for many writers of the Celtic literary Revival in Ireland. The Dublin Theosophical Lodge was founded in 1886 since then the ideas of Celtic Revival and theosophy have flown together and persons like AE and James Cousins are by-products of this new interest.

11. Chap. 4 : The Occult and the Modern World, p. 66.

CHAPTER - III

THE IRISH LITERARY REVIVAL

Various impulses towards a revival of the Celtic religion and culture were active from the middle of the nineteenth Century. The pioneer investigator on this subject was the French philosopher and writer Ernest Renan (1823-92) whose "La Poesie des Races Celtiques" (The Poetry of the Celtic Races) was published in 1856. Reman's essay had a profound impact on Matthew Arnold who elaborated Renan's remarks on the Celtic element in Literature in his famous work *Lectures on the Study of Celtic Literature* (1867). Here Arnold argued that England might recover from middle class "Philistinism" under the influence of the newly discovered "Celtic genuis". He says :

> Now, then, is the moment for the greater delicacy and *spirituality of the Celtic Peoples* who are blended with us, if it be but wisely directed to make itself prized and honoured.[1]
>
> —(emphasis mine)

By emphasizing on the "Spirituality" of Celtic Culture Arnold created an idealized image of the Celt that ultimately were of immense value to the leaders of the Irish Literary Revival. William Sharp (Fiona Mcleod), a noted Celtic Revivalist, emphasizing Renan and Arnold's contribution to the Celtic Revival rightly observed :

> Renan's essay in France and Germnay and Matthew Arnold's in his country and America were the torches which have lit so many Celtic brands.[2]

1. *Matthew Arnold, Lectures and Essays in Criticism,* ed. R.H. Super (The University of Michigan, 1962), p. 390.
2. William Sharp : *Papers Critical and Reminiscent* (London, 1912), p. 4.

He also said that the essays of Renan and Arnold "were like two winds which fanned the Celtic flames which is now one of the most potent influences in contemporary Literature".

To be sure, Arnold had not expected or desired a Celtic Revival. He only wanted the Celts fully to enter into the Anglo-Saxon Cultural main stream.

Matthew Arnold and later William Morris who criticised British materialism from within, saw in the Celtic ethos a principle of spiritual health akin to their ideals. From the later half of the nineteenth Century, a large number of scholars, poets and writers devoted themselves to the recovery of the Celtic heritage. Among them was Douglas Hyde (1860-1949) who worked for the revival of the Gaelic. He founded the Gaelic League in 1893 to promote the de-anglicizing wave and sought to create an awareness of the richness of this Celtic language. He translated some of the gems of old Irish Literature available both orally and in written Gaelic; among them which deserve special mention were *Beside the Fire : A Collection of Irish Gaelic Folk Stories* (1890) and *Love Songs of Connaught* (1893).

In mid-nineteenth century Ireland some Irish Poets such as Mangan and Ferguson and to a lesser extent, Aubrey de vere, helped initiate the true impulses of the Celtic Revival.[3] They moved closer to their national heritage and created in verse and prose image after image of the legendary greatness of their people. They translated the ancient literature of the Gael and revived in literature the most characteristic elements of the Celtic spirits i.e. the sense of the mystery and the mystical yearning for the Infinite which forms the Central focus of the poets and writers of the Irish Literary Revival. Ferguson's *Lays of the Western Gael* (1864) in particular, the first work of any length to deal with the epic cycles of Ireland, may be said to be an attempt towards the revivification of the Celtic Spirit. Another important contribution towards redefining the Celtic character and in restoration of the ancient Celtic heritage came from Standish O'Grady's *History of Ireland : Heroic Period* (1878-1880).

---

3. *The World of W.B. Yeats*, ed. Robin Skelton and Ann Saddlemyer (University of Washington Press, 1965), p. 28.

This work was of seminal importance in fostering the idealized image of the Celtic tradition. AE who appreciated the heroic grandeur of O'Grady's tales described his own feelings upon first reading O'Grady :

> I felt like a man who suddenly feels ancient memories rushing at him and knows he was born in a royal house.[4]

It was not only AE but also most of the writers of the Irish Literary Revival who testify to O'Grady's influence as being so strong as to make him "the father of the Irish Renaissance."

At the end of the eighties and the beginning of the nineties great advances were made in the field of Comparative Philosophy and religion which made a tremendous impact and contributed to the dissolution of the mystery or uniqueness of Christian Church. As Madam Blavatsky put it, "the Church has two far mightier enemies than the 'heretics' and the 'Infidels', and these are Comparative Mythology and Philology."[5]

Philologists pointed out that Sanskrit, Greek and Gaelic were sister tongues of the great Aryan language group and Comparative mythologists point out remarkable parallels in the cultural patterns of the ancient Aryan Cultures. The publication of the writings of John Rhys and Henry de Jubainville were influential in this issue. Their comparative study of the religions of the world led the writers of the Irish Literary Revival to a recognition of the Wisdom Religion of India. They found that many of the beliefs and practices of Celtic religion practised under Druid Priests were similar to those of ancient Indian Culture, thus indicating an ancient common link. John Rhys in his Hibbert Lectures (1886) showed how some of the principal figures in the mythology of the Greeks and the other Aryans had their counterpart in the theology of the ancient Celts. Rhys then compared the Celtic culture hero Guidon (Mercury) with the Hindu God Indra. Finally he guessed at Celtic cosmogony and theogony as part of a primordial Aryan myth. Henry de Jubainville, the best equipped and most esteemed among the Celtic

---

4. 'A Tribute to Standish O'Grady', in *Standish O'Grady : The Man and the Writer,* ed. Hugh Art O'Grady (Dublin : The Talbot Press, 1929), p. 72.
5. *Isis Unveiled,* vol. II, p. 30.

scholars of this period, virtually said the same thing in his book *The Irish Mythological Cycle and Celtic Mythology* (1903).

These lectures on comparative religion provoked a widespread discussion. They rekindled an interest in the ancient myths and legends of the country. They showed that it was through myths that the ancient man said all he knew about God and man's soul. "Though turned into old wives tale, the myths really told us", noted Yeats, "of once famous religion, and they were still luminous from the rosy dawn of human revery". AE in his dedication to his poetical work, *The House of the Titans* calls myths, "the scripture of the world". He further says :

> These myths were born out of the spirit of man, and drew their meaning from that unplumbed profundity. I think in after ages they will speak to us with deeper voices and meanings.[6]

This unravelling of the deeper voices and meanings inherent in the mythologies of the world were the subject matter of most of the writings of Madam Blavatsky. That all mythologies and folk lores had a deep symbolic meaning and a common spiritual basis was one of the fundamental doctrines of Madam Blavatsky's Theosophical works. The writers of the Irish Literary Revival carried with them the same kind of conviction about myths of the past. The research of the Celtic scholars corroborated much of what one finds in *The Secret Doctrine* of Blavatsky. Poets of the Irish Literary Revival found that the beliefs prevalent in Hindu tradition, and among the Greeks in Homer's time, were essentially those held by the ancient Druids. They discovered that Madam Blavatsky in her *Isis Unveiled* sought to trace the fundamental similarity of myths and folklores of the Celtic, semitic and Aryan families. The similarity of the myths of various countries in the Occident and the Orient shown by Madam Blavatsky led Yeats and AE to symbolical readings of the ancient Irish myths in terms of theosophy.

Both of them made a search for organic connection between theosophy and the occult lores of the East and the Irish tradition. They linked up the natural mysticism of the Celt with theosophy. Both of them thought that Madam Blavatsky and her movement

---

6. Cited by Cousins. See his 'Preface' to *The Hound of Uladh* (Madras, India, 1942), p. 70.

anticipated a new age of spiritual recovery from the crude materialism of the Post-Darwinian epoch.

Theosophy thus became a source of vital inspiration for a group of writers of the Irish Literary Revival.[7] Their literary activities were accompanied by some stimulation of the religious instinct. John Eglinton in his *A Memoir of AE* (1937) gives a vivid account of the excitement caused by the Theosophical Movement among the Irish writers of the Revival. He says :

> Probably there has never been in any country a period of literary activity which has not been preceded or accompanied by some stimulation of the religious interest. Any one in search of this in Ireland at this time may find it if he looks for it, though he certainly will not find it in either the Catholic or the various protestant religious bodies, he will find it.... in the ferment caused in the minds of a group of youngmen by the early activities of the Theosophical Movement in Dublin (p.1).

This group of youngmen who were the leading figures of the Theosophical Movement were Yeats, Charles Johnston, C.F. Wright, George William Russell (AE), Charles Week, John Eglinton, James Cousins and others. These young pioneers saturated themselves in the wisdom literature of India which came to them through the channels of theosophy. This interest in Indian thought led Yeats' class fellow Charles Johnston, a classical scholar of Trinity College, Dublin, to read Sanskrit instead of Greek and Latin. Johnston translated the *Upanishads* and presented a commentary of his own on this subject. This volume on Indian Scripture is called *From the Upanishads* which was published in 1885. his second volume *The Crest Jewel of Wisdom* is a translation from the *Bhagwad Gita*. Johnston dedicated the former volume to AE, the companion of his first adventure in Theosophy. As one of the initiators of the Dublin Theosophical Group, Johnston realized the importance of the message of Indian thought for his time. He admitted that this knowledge of Oriental wisdom came at a critical period in Europe's intellectual history when its ecclesiastical

7. See W. Emmett Small : 'H.P. Blavatsky's Influence on Ireland's Literary Renaissance' in *H.P. Blavatsky and the Secret Doctrine* ed. Virginia Hanson (The Theosophical Publishing House, Adyar, Madras, India, 1971), p. 108.

fabrics, built through several centuries was beginning to look inadequate. He believed that this tide of Oriental thought was going to create new waves of thought in Ireland.[8] He seems to be inspired by the following insight of Madam Blavatsky, who says :

> Who knows but that as the Christian Church has unconsciously begotten free thought by reaction against her own cruelty, rapacity and dogmaticism, the public mind may be glad to *follow the lead of the Orientalists away from Jerusalem and towards Ellora; and that then much more will be discovered that is now hidden.*[9]
>
> (emphasis mine)

"India", Blavatsky regarded as "the Almamater, not only of the civilizations, arts and sciences but also of all the great religions of antiquity.[10]

It was not only Johnston but Yeats, AE, Cousins and a host of other Irish writers who felt inspired by this tide of Oriental thought. This is emphasized by Herbert Howarth in his book *The Irish Writers, 1880-1940* (1958) thus :

> All the poets of the Irish Literary Movement, with Mangam as their forerunner, asked the Orient to give them something : AE asked for authority and intuitions, Yeats for the trappings of a system, Joyce for the polar opposite of his intellect.[11]

The greatest channel of theosophical influence was Madam Blavatsky and most of the Irish writers of the Revival directly or indirectly acknowledge Madam Blavatsky's influence. Charles Johnston, for instance, who became the key figure in the Theosophical circle in Ireland, writes :

> Far greater is the value of her spiritual teaching, she outlined the path of Immortal life, indicating the sign posts of immemorial way.[12]

---

8. See Johnston 'Sanskrit Study in the West' in *Theosophical Quarterly* (New York), Vol. 29, Year 1931-32, p. 337.
9. *Isis Unveiled* (1877), Vol. II, p. 26.
10. Ibid., p. 30. She wrote a long chapter entitled 'India the cradle of race' in her book *Isis Unveiled* (Vol. I), See Chap. XV.
11. Herbert Howarth : 'James Joyce' *The Irish Writers, 1880-1940* (London, 1958), p. 262.
12. See Charles Johnston's essay 'on H.P.B.' in the *Theosophical Quarterly*, Vol. 29, 1931-32.

Johnston founded the Dublin Theosophical Lodge in April 1886 at Ely Place which became one of the important literary centres during the last decade of the nineteenth and the beginning of the twentieth century. Prof. Edmund Curtis (1881-1943), an Irish historian and a scholar of modern history, described the Lodge's exquisite decor and thought - the refined cultural conversations of the sitters could have rivalled that of a Paris Sallon.[13] It thus became a nursery of literary and philosophic talents and offered an intellectual platform for the Irish nationalists who sought to align Theosophy with Druidic religious tradition. W.B. Yeats has pointed out with characteristic enthusiasm of the period that "it (the Dublin Lodge) had produced more (talents) in literature than Trinity College in its three centuries." C.J. Ryan has also noted the importance of the Dublin Theosophical Lodge in the moulding of the Irish Literary Revival in his book, *H.P. Blavatsky and the Theosophical Movement* (1975).[14] Other testimonies to this influence of the Dublin Theosophical Lodge can be found in the Irish-American Critic, Ernest Boyd's Book, *Ireland's Literary Renaissance* (1922). Appreciating the literary qualities of the Journals published by the Dublin Theosophists (1892-1897) Boyd remarks :

> Their Journals, *The Irish Theosophist, The Internationalist* and *The International Theosophist* contain a great deal of matter which has long since taken a high place in Modern Anglo-Irish Literature. It was in the pages of those reviews that the first poems of "AE" were published, and to them we owe a great number of Essays afterwards collected by John Eglinton under the title, *Pebbles from the Brook.*[15]

Sean O'Faolin (1900 -), a modern Irish writer and critic says that "Anglo-Irish Literature rose out of the ancestral memory,"[16] and the Theosophical Movement in Ireland played an important role in the awakening of this 'ancestral memory'. The Theosophical Movement also added depth to the Irish Literary Revival by providing an Oriental spiritual background to its national revivalist work.

---

13. Summerfield, p. 53.
14. *Ibid.*, See p. 275.
15. Boyd : 'AE Mystic and Economist', *Appreciation and Depreciation* (Dublin, 1918), p. 26.
16. *The Irish* (1980), p. 131.

II

As we review the history of the Theosophical Movement in Ireland the name of George William Russell (AE) assumes considerable importance. AE, the first two letters of the Gnostic word AEON, meaning heavenly Spirit, was the pen name of George William Russell. W.B. Yeats in his *Autobiographies* (p. 239) says that George Russell was in the eyes of the community, a Saint and a genius. Yeats has acknowledged Russell as the leader of mystical thought in Dublin. He says that "Russell became... the one masterful influence among young Dublin men and women who love religious speculation, but have no historic faith." Russell was regarded as the 'Socrates of Dublin'. He was one of those personalities who was always spoken of with respect and affection. Monk Gibbon, an eminent modern Irish Critic, says that 'Russell is the nearest thing Ireland has ever had to a prophet'.[17]

Yeats was quite aware of these aspects of Russell's character. In one of his letters Yeats writes : "Dublin is waking up in a number of ways and about a number of things. Russell is doing a good part in the awakening."[18] James H. Cousins, one of the younger participants of the Irish Literary Revival, has called Russell a father figure of Irish Literary Renaissance. He added that "AE had been one of the founders of the first Lodge of the Theosophical Society in Dublin and was in my time the chief exponent in Ireland of Theosophical experience and thought.[19]

Russell believed that the Theosophical Philosophy which was primarily based on Eastern religious thought could provide an answer to the contemporary religious problems. He built his ideas of a new renaissance on the discovery of the East. He says :

> If Europe is to have a renaissance comparable with that which came from the wedding of Christianity with the Greek and

17. See W.R. Rodger : *Irish Literary Portraits* (London, 1972), p. 185.
18. *The Letters of W.B. Yeats,* ed. Allan Wade (New York, 1954), p. 306. (Dec. 25, 1898).
19. *We Two Together,* p. 110.

> Latin cultures it must, I think come from a second wedding of Christianity with the culture of the East.[20]

In his spiritual autobiography, *The Candle of Vision* (1918), Russell says :

> Our religions make promises to be fulfilled beyond the grave because they have no knowledge now to be put to the test, but the ancients speak of a divine vision to be attained while we are yet in the body (p.20).

What Russell wants to suggest here is that Theosophy or the 'Wisdom of the ancient' is more useful for spiritual solace than Christianity. It does not console man with a vain hope of salvation after death but strongly affirms that man can attain his godhood here and now. It does not separate man and God in a fixed duality. Russell advises his readers to mistrust a religion which does not help to attain divinity. He says that the messengers of this false religon are the prophets of darkness. In one of his letters to Van Wyck Brooks he writes : "our religions are outworn and we must find cultural substitute".[21] This substitute Russell seemed to have found in the wisdom religion of India which was largely employed by Theosophy and sought to offer an alternative to orthodox Christianity. He saw the main object of his life to be the spread of Oriental teaching expressed in Theosophy.

Theosophy had a considerable influence in the restoration of respectability about the Celtic myths and legends. Russell attempted a new interpretation of Irish lores in the analogy of Theosophy in his autobiography, *The Candle of Vision.* The title of the book is revelatory : Theosophy was the light of the candle which led him through the dark passages of the Celtic past.

Russell's stories in his book *Imaginations and Reveries* (1915) reveal an intuition of weaving Orientalism and Celticism together. They range from "the Cave of Lilith" to "The Meditations of Ananda", with Oriental theme and to "A Dream of Angus Oge" with its definite Celtic material. In his "The Meditations of Ananda" Russell portrays Ananda's experience of meditation in a vivid and

---

20. See Raynor C. Johnson : 'AE' in *The Light and the Gate* (1964), p. 5.
21. Ibid.

most suggestive manner. The story begins with the picture of an ascetic who has just been awakened from profound meditation under the banyan tree. Russell describes Ananda's experience in the following terms :

> All day long before his inner eye burned the 'light of the Lokas'[22] until he was wearied and exhausted with their splendours. Space glowed like a diamond with intolerable lustre and there was no end to the dazzling processions of figures. He saw how those orbs were held within luminous orbs of wider circuit; and vaster and vaster grew the vistas, until atlast he bore the burden of immeasurable worlds. Seeing for Brahma he found only the great illusion as Brahma's being.

The above excerpt shows how Russell understood the nature of mystical vision found in ancient Indian literature. This may be compared with Russell's own experiences in the following passage : "When our lamp is lit, we find the house of our being has many chambers and creatures live there who come and go,....[23] Ananda's visions of many luminous orbs and the growing vastness of the vistas before his eyes seem to be quite similar to that of Russell's own experiences of expansive modes of vision he enumerates in *The Candle of Vision.*

"The Midnight Blossom", another story of *Imaginations and Reveries*, also deals with an Oriental theme. The story seems to have been based on Madam Blavatsky's short treatise, *The Voice of Silence* which tells us Buddha's story of renunciation of the bliss or Nirvana to enlighten others. By 'midnight blossom' Russell means 'Earth's signal fires' which she puts forth to receive her Masters or the realized souls - when they are born to this world. In a dark night Russell has a vision of the 'midnight blossom' and he exclaims in great joy :

> Brothers ! Masters ! look ! the wonderful things ! And another, and yet another ! we looked and saw the holy blossom, the midnight flower ... we remained long long in silence, looking at the sacred flower.

---

22. 'Lokas' is a theosophical term meaning heavenly regions.
23. *The Candle of Vision,* p. 53.

All these stories reflect the intimations of spiritual vision the sanction for which he derived from Theosophical literatures. Another story called "The story of a star" offers the fundamental teaching of the *Upanishads.* To the question - 'To what end is this life poured forth and withdrawn ?' The answer comes : 'The end is creation and creation is joy'. Speaking about his distinctive note in Russell's writings George Moore has quite rightly said that "the 'Upanishads' and the 'vedas' were born again in verse and in prose in the writings of Russell".

It is these ideas of the wisdom religion of India that led Russell to wander at night murmuring the 'Ineffable Name' OM to himself with the reverence of a mystic. Russell gives an account of such nocturnal wanderings in *The Candle of Vision* (p. 118). He says if he is asked to tell the purpose of such method of spiritual exercise (murmuring the Ineffable Name OM to oneself) he would say that : "he was trying to put himself in the place of his Aryan ancestors - affirming thus that his celtic ancestors and the Aryans were one.

Russell has presented this subject in a poem called "OM" which shows the poet's direct contact with the wisdom religion of India. In this poem a brahmin boy is seen to be chanting the word OM in an Indian vale at dawn. The boy murmurs the holy sound with a tender heart, and his eyes glow like the morning sun in expectation of a communion with Brahma or the 'Ancestral Self'. OM is the beginning and the end of the universe.

> The word which Brahma at his dawn
> Outbreathes and endeth at his night,
> Whose tide of sounds go rolling on
> Gives birth to orbs of pearly light[24]

In another poem called "Indian" Russell portrays the same glory and splendour of Brahma who 'dreams the joy that throng in space', that is, he is the sole repository of truths of existence. Russell seems to imply that this is the kind of instinctive faith that reverberates in the soil of India.

That Russell was soaked in the wisdom religion of India is evident in many of his poems. In "Evanescence" he echoes the famous Upanishadic dictum *Tat - Tvam Asi* or "That Thou Art":

24. AE: *Collected Poems* (Macmillan, London 1920), p. 155.

> Could you and I when e'er the light appears
> Cry at the wonder, "I am that", as did the vedic sages?

His poem called "The Robing of the King" presents his regret that he could not prepare for death like an Indian Yogi 'leaving the body as he chose' instead of being thrust out of it.

As a genuine mystic Russell affirms that man is capable of spiritual ascension through vision. For there is an essential divinity in man which at times becomes conscious of itself and feel at one with all souls. This absorption of the self into the Universal Soul is the fundamental tenet of Theosophy and is affirmed by the mystics of all ages.

Russell deplores the degrading state of modern man in a mechanised unspiritual society almost in the tone of Blavatsky. He gives us a clue of his spiritual vision in the following statements:

> I would cry out to our humanity, sinking deeper into our Iron Age, that the Golden world is about us and that beauty is open to all, and none are shut out from it who will turn to and seek for it.[25]

It is this note of strong protest against materialism and an affirmation of a new hope of spiritual revival in the writings of Madam Blavatsky from which Russell and Cousins drew inspiration. In an essay on "Tidal wave" Blavatsky also puts this new hope in the following terms:

> The great psychic and spiritual change now taking place in the realm of human soul, is quite remarkable verily the spirit of man is atlast awakened.[26]

She further says that the premonition of this spiritual awakening is made apparent to us by many creative writers who have arisen to defend the right of the spirit to reign over matter. She says that "many are the honest aspiring souls now raising themselves like a dead wall against the torrent of the muddy waters of Materialism.[27] Russell who is one of such 'honest and aspiring souls' expressed his

25. *The Candle of Vision*, p. 34.
26. See *Lucifer* (London) Vol. V. 1890, reprinted in *Adyar Library Bulletin*, 'Blavatsky Number', Nov. 1942.
27. Ibid.

revulsion against the mechanization of life and society of the modern period. His social work was inspired by such hope and faith. He wanted to build up a Co-operative Commonwealth in Ireland insisting on the emergence of a rural civilization which would be free from the competition of the modern materialistic age. An instinctive Theosophist and an Irish nationalist, Russell wrote in the hope of helping to create a synthesis of spirituality, a breadth of culture, and of the national tradition in Ireland.

Russell's most influential poetical collection was *Homeward : Songs by the Way* (1894). Yeats commenting on the poems said that they established Russell (AE) as a leader of the spiritual movement of Ireland. As early as 1891 he had called AE an "Irish Visionary", and from the day the *Homeward* (which bore as a Preface to the statement "I know I am a spirit") was published, he became for Yeats the centre of the "Spiritual group" of Irish writers, and was given primacy of place in almost all his references to such a group.[28] The Poems of *Homeward : Songs by the Way* were first published in *The Irish Theosophist*. 'Home' to Russell means the Platonic or Wordsworthian faith in the return of the soul to its source, the absorption of the spirit in the universal spirit. As Cousins put it, "Russell is mainly preoccupied with the homeward process".[29] The poems in this volume are the records of ecstasies which mark the search of the soul for the Infinite. In the poem called "Desire" for instance, we see the poet's mystical yearning for the Invisible.

> And with what yearning inexpressible,
> Rising from long forgetfulness I turn
> To thee, invisible,....[30]

This spirit of turning to invisible or God is also expressed in the poem "Star Teachers". Here the poet looks at the starry sky and feels:

> These myriad eyes that look on me are mine;
> Wandering beneath them I have found again

---

28. See Phillip Marcus : *Yeats and the beginning of the Irish Renaissance* (Cornell University Press, 1970), p. 182.
29. *New Ways in English Literature* (1917), p. 49.
30. *Collected Poems*, p. 22.

> The ancient ample moment, the divine,
> The God-root within man.[31]

To seek and realize this god-root within man is the fundamental quest of Russell as it is to all mystics.

But Russell's poems lack breadth of experience they seek to distill. Yeats pointed this out. He also found in Russell wanting a lack of awareness of the power of the evil. His poetry reads like a poetry of abstractions where the essence was kept and the dross of experience was emptied out. Because of his essential absorption of Theosophical thought evil ceases to be a problem with Russell. In the theosophical ways of thought evil is only a perversion of knowledge. On the question of evil Russell says in his essay called "Religion and love" reflecting an attitude to life, "that the greatest evil of all is not to be able to see the divine everywhere". This is what is called 'Avidya' or perversion of knowledge in Hindu thought. Theosophical thought remained the staple and source of sustenance in all Russell's writings. Monk Gibbon, a modern Irish critic, has made this point clear. He says that :

> Theosophy did for Russell what the Classics do for other men, that it stood for a background of culture in his life as well as representing much hard work and mental discipline.[32]

---

31. Ibid., p. 15.
32. *The Living Torch* (1937) also cited in Abinas Bose: *Three Mystic Poets*, Kolhapur, 1945, Chap. 'A Poet of Theosophy', p. 65.

CHAPTER - IV

COUSINS AS A POET AND PLAYWRIGHT

We have mentioned earlier that Cousins started his poetic and dramatic career under the direct inspiration of the Dublin Theosophical Movement and the Irish Literary Revival. Most of his early poems and plays which were written from 1894 to 1915 reflect this dual heritage. He wrote several poems even after he left Ireland and settled in India in 1915. He continued to write poetry and plays till the late forties. He published almost twenty volumes of poetical works. He wrote poems of various kinds, mystical and visionary, poems of Celtic myth and legends, poems of patriotic feeling, and of love and nature. Behind all them, his primary concern, as he himself puts it in one of his poems called "The Theme", is :

I sing of waters, winds and trees—
But no ! I do not sing of these.
One theme alone my Daemon sings :-
The spirit mixed in mortal things.
She sings no passing wind or tree :
She sings the haunting mystery.[1]

That is, Cousins looks at the world as two dimensional reality both material and spiritual - and all intertwined in 'spirit mixed in mortal things'. His poems are attempts to capture the essence of things - the 'haunting mystery' of life and experience. His early poetry, *The Voice of One* (1900), *The Quest* (1906), *The Awakening* (1907) all with their mystical titles, embody this spirit of mysticism. Most of them achieve a fine blend of Theosophy and the nostalgia for the spirit of the Irish Literary Revival. They also try to convey the unrest of the soul of the poet and his yearning to attain the consciousness of unity and mystery of life and the universe.

---

1. *Collected Poems*, p. 278.

The title piece of Cousins' 'first serious volume' of poems, "The Voice of One" for instance, is a monologue representing a remorseful soul seeking spiritual freedom. The late Victorian melancholy and spiritual despair can be heard when the speaker laments :

And I have seen my fairy gold
Turn all to dull misshapen lead;
And hungry I have been, and cold,
And wished me harboured with the dead.[2]

The poet's realisation that he has failed to fulfil his inner spiritual potentialities led him to this regret and he laments that his life has become as dull and heavy as a piece of lead. The second stanza of the poem reinforces this note of spiritual despair :

Through mighty issues I have slept -
And waked to unmomentous ends :

This suggests that the poet is suffering from a sense of spiritual inadequacy. It is the same kind of feeling we come across among the Romantic poets about the deadening of their inspiration. Love's mysterious star beckons him from far away; in his dream he sees the star infinitely near yet when he awakes he experiences an unbridgeable gulf between his dream and reality, aspiration and achievement. A typical romantic dilemma again is expressed. The poet finds everyday life inadequate and uninteresting. He therefore yearns for an innocent freedom beyond worldly experience :

And sometimes I have longed to free
My soul from all that stains and mars,
To taste the quiet in the sea,
The peace that lodges with the stars.

Here is finely caught the tone which is essentially Celtic. The poet's longing to free his soul from 'all that stains and mars' suggests his longing for disentanglement from the material world, and desire for the loneliness of the spirit.

This yearning for mystical experience is adequately conveyed against the twilight background of the evening and the early hours

---

2. *Collected Poems,* p. 1.

of the dawn. When the twilight descends, the poet finds the world permeated with mystery :

> Lo ! I have stood besides the deep;
> And I have watched the twilight skies
> Grow grey with mystery and sleep,
> ... .
> And I have heard strange voices speak
> In words half-uttered, half-withdrawn,
> While far away a mountain peak
> Put on the vestments of the dawn;[3]

The lines suggest the poet's subjective experiences in terms of natural background. Twilight and dawn bring to the poet a sense of mystery and the other world, and strange voices speak 'words half-uttered and half-withdrawn' suggest the intangible truth of mystical experience. The Celtic belief in 'Sidhes' who are believed to come out of the secret places in twilight to communicate with human beings is being echoed here. Traditionally the Irish believed that the world of man and the world of fairies or the supernatural do not stand at opposite poles. Both these worlds coexist and meet in the half light of twilight or dawn. The twilight adorns the world with mystery and spirituality and Cousins conceives it as hallowed by the presence of the 'Great Silence', a theosophical term meaning the Divine Being.

The poet's intense longing for the mystery of the universe makes him exclaim in the paradoxical terms of a mystic :

> ... ...
> And, seeing not, I yearn for sight
> To read the heart of praise or blame,
> To catch the beam within the light.
> And feel the fire behind the flame;[4]

He seeks a safe anchorage in the world of innocence where he could 'pluck immortal flowers' and 'bathe in a cool clear flood'. Finally he attains a realization :

---

3. *Collected Poems*, p. 5.
4. *Collected Poems,* p. 3.

And know that thing for which I seek
....
And turn Truth's never-ceasing wheel,
And from its distaff spin my thread.

The poem combines the height of poet's spiritual aspiration with his awareness of the unhappy plight of man's life which is a strenuous struggle with fate - we turn truth's never ceasing wheel - we are fated to work but achievement is not within our grasp.

This melancholy tone is overcome in a poem called "A drift in Moonlight" which celebrates a boating party over the river Lee. Here the poet seems to attain a state of spiritual joy :

In such an hour as this the soul
Shakes free from sense that cloys,
And sights after her starry goal,
And thrills to nobler joys -
Than those vouchsafed which lithesome limbs
Danced to impassioned Paphian hymns.[5]

The poet thinks that the experience of spiritual joy is nobler than the sensual experiences celebrated in Paphian hymns of the devotees of Venus, in the Island of Paphos. The idea is that spiritual joy is unencumbered with any limitations or satiety. Describing this blessed stated he exclaims :

From such rare hours - as brief as few
Our dearest hope is this :
To win an ample voice and view,
To draw a deeper bliss,
And hear reverberate through our dreams
The thunder of Immortal themes.[6]

A passionate yearning to achieve this 'deeper bliss' is expressed in the poet's meditation in a deep quietude beside a stream in another poem called "Vision". The poem is a sonnet.

When I from life's unrest had earned the grace
Of utter ease beside a quiet stream ;
When all that was had mingled in a dream

5. *Collected Poems*, p. 12.
6. *Ibid*, p. 5.

To eyes awakened out of time and place;
Then in the cup of the great moment's space
Was crushed the living wine from things that seem;
I drank the joy of every Beauty's gleam,
And saw God's glory face to shining face.

Almost my brow was chastened to the ground,
But for an inner voice that said : Arise
Wisdom is wisdom only to the wise.
Thou art thyself the Royal thou hast crowned :
In Beauty thine own Beauty thou hast found,
And thou hast looked on God with God's own eyes.[7]

Here the poet has been able to overcome the sense of duality and like a true mystic realizes the identity of God and man. In the Beauty of God he finds the enlarged reflection of his own image echoing *the atman is Brahma* of Indian scriptures. Cousins had earned the reputation of a mystic poet who could remarkably combine Eastern and Western modes of mysticism. So two of his poems were included in the *Oxford Book of Mystical Verse* (1917). The second poem called "Quest", embodies the poet's quest for ideal beauty; someone in whose eyes he may find 'healing for life's smart'. Like "Vision" quoted above, this is also a short poem and can be quoted in full :

They said : She dwelleth in some place apart,
Immortal Truth, within whose eyes
Who looks may find the secret of the skies
And healing for life's smart !
I sought her in long caverns underground,
On heights where lightnings flashed and fell ;
I scaled high Heaven; I stormed the gates of Hell,
But her I never found -
Till thr' the tumults of my quest and caught
A whisper; Here, within thy heart,
I dwell ; for I am thou : behold thou art
The seeker - and the sought.[8]

---

7. *The Oxford Book of Mystical Verse,* Ed. Nicholson and Lee, (Oxford Clarendan Press, 1916), p.585.
8. *The Oxford Book of Mystical Verse,* Ed. Nicholson & Lee, (Oxford Clarendan Press, 1916), p. 584.

This mystical attitude is also quite familiar in the tradition of East and West - 'God is within us' not in 'Caverns under ground' or in some place apart. The unseen universal spirit working through life and nature is a familiar assumption in Romantic poetry and notably in Shelley. When the poet gets tired after his search for the ideal in far away places he hears the whisper of affirmation from within - 'within thy heart I dwell'. This poem echoes a typical Upanishadic formula - *Tat Tvam Asi* : 'That thou art'. The idea underlining the poem is a basic theosophical truth - the affirmation of the identity between the seeker and the sought - the subject and the object.

The poet carries on this theme of spiritual awakening in another poem called "Awake" :

> From a sleep I emerge : I am clothed again by this woven vesture of laws ;—
> But I am not, never again shall be the man that I was.
> At the zenith of life I am born again. I begin.
> Know ye, I am awake, outside and within.[9]

This experience of a spiritual birth or awakening provides the poet with a new confidence and this assertion rings clearly in the following lines reminiscent of the *Bhagwad Gita* :

> I have flung away the body's prison rug. -
> I have burst the cobweb haunted chamber, the mind.
> I have sent three shouts of freedom along with wind.
> I have struck one hand of kinship in the hands of Gods,
> and one in the hands of women and men.
> I am awake ! I shall never sleep again ![10]

The poet has emerged out of his physical existence; the word 'Prison rug; seems to echo a sense of the *Bhagwad Gita* where the bodily existence is compared to that of an 'worn-out garment' (Ch. II, V. 22).

As a result of this spiritual awakening the poet feels a kinship not only with Gods, but with all men and women as well, and becomes a votary of universal brotherhood. This poem was appreciated by Cousins' mentor AE who sent a brief note on the poem to Cousins. AE says : "The poem you call "Awake" presents a

---

9. *Collected Poems*, p. 134.
10. Ibid., p. 135.

true ideal with real power. I like especially those lines with the recurrent idea, 'The deafness that men call hearing/This blindness that men call sight' - these are extraordinarily good".

These poems made a considerable impression on the literary scene in Ireland. Mary Sturgeon, a contemporary critic of modern English poetry, commended this poem particularly and said that it was a characteristic contribution of the 'Irish School'. This trend of blending of Irish tone and Indian theosophical thought is the most notable contribution of Cousins' poetry. Mary Sturgeon hints at Cousins' special qualification to make this spiritual affirmation because she knows that Cousins has found a more positive faith than many of his contemporaries. She says :

> But significantly the latest poetic utterance of Ireland is a cry of complete realization. It has remained for Cousins to hear the call of his age more consciously than his compatriots; and is left to him in grace and courage, to declare it: 'From a sleep I emerge ... I am awake, I shall never sleep again.[11]

It is Cousins' theosophical initiation that has brought to him this firm realization of being 'twice born', even assuming a new kind of name called 'Jay Ram'.

Apart from these mystical and visionary poems Cousins, like most of his compatriots, devoted his poetic faculties to sing the beauty and glory of Ireland. Most of these poems were written in the first flush of patriotic enthusiasm and they celebrated the uniqueness of Irish life and landscape. Among these poems "The Twelve Bens", "Slieve Cullen", "Scrabo Rock" and "To Eire" may be mentioned. 'Ben' in Gaelic means peaks. In this poem the poet celebrates the solemn beauty of the mountains of Connemara which, like Yeats' 'Sligo', is one of the most beautiful places in Ireland. Cousins' poetic power in description and invocation of scenic beauty can be seen in these poems. For instance :

> Here limpid lark - streams trickle down
> A hundred peaks of song ;
> There, silent sheep and lambkins lie,

---

11. See Chap. 'Irish School', *Contemporary Poets* (Harrap, London, 1920), p. 153.

A white, uncertain thing,
Like lingering snow that fain would spy
The secret of the spring.[12]

This creates a vivid scene of early Spring when new born lambs lie scattered on mountain slopes creating a semblance of snow - that has now yet melted as if wants to discover the secret of the spring. It shows a genuine love for country scenes - and touches us with the freshness of a vision. Similarly "A Donegal Sketch", "Optimism - Galway Style", "A Flail Song", "After Grass", "Frocken Gathering", "In Praise of Country life", "A Gypsy Dance in Kerry", "Why the Grass is short in Connemara" - all these poems provide us with an intimate sense of things. The poet's renderings of Irish peasant life deserve also special mention. "Flail Song", one of these poems, conveys the living rhythm of harvesting songs of the Irish farmers :

Now scythe and spade aside are laid,
And autumn shade will soon be here :
Come, fetch the flail down from its nail,
And fill the pail with water clear.
See , all the floor is covered o'er.
With goldened store of ripened grain.
Now, take your places left and right,
And swing and smite with might and main.[13]

Vivid details of the harvesting operation is described here. The rhythm of the poem succeeds in capturing the tone of folksongs. These poems on Irish life and landscape strike us for their simplicity of subject and diction.

Cousins' poems on Celtic myths and legends combine his national and patriotic sentiments with theosophical reflections. His shorter lyric, "The Bell Branch", which is one of the representative poems of the Celtic Twilight School, achieves this synthesis. It opens in the following manner :

[14]*Shoheen, Sho ho*
Birds are homeward winging

12. *Collected Poems,* p. 6.
13. *Collected Poems,* p. 65.
14. An instinctive exclamation of Irish country people used to frighten or drive away fowls.

Shoheen, Sho ho
Herdsmen on the hills are singing :
Short the night and long the day
Come ye weary flocks away.
Folded in deep shadows drowse.
And on long sweet grasses browse
Where the murmuring waters flow
Shoheen, Sho ho
Hark, the Bell - branch ringing !
Danaans from the hills are singing.

The 'Bell-branch' is a device of the Irish fairies, to call mortals away from material allegiance. Cousins has used this myth to suggest the call of the spirit to urge human beings away from their material life. The refrain in Gaelic *Shoheen, Sho ho* creates a hypnotic effect in the poem. The tone of the poem is very much like those of AE's "Carrowmore" and Yeats' "Stolen Child". The concluding lines of the poem seem to echo them :

Time is old and earth is grey
Come ye weary ones away.
Where with white untroubled brows
The Immortals dream and drowse
And the streams of quiet flow
Shoheen, Sho ho.

Most of the poems in the *Bell Branch* (1970) breathe this typically Celtic Spirit. Ernest A Boyd, a critic and historian of Irish literature, while discussing Yeats' early poetic drama, *The Land of Hearts' Desire,* remarks that it is not only Yeats who has often sung this longing of a soul for the beyond but many other Irish poets like Nora Hopper in her *Fairy Music* and James Cousins, in *The Bell Branch.*[15] Boyd observes that most of Cousins' poems in *The Bell Branch* embody an escape from the tedium of human life into a fairy land, a characteristic Celtic Revivalist mode. The religious and mystic fervour of Cousins leads him to invent Celtic mythological subjects with such mystical significance.

---

15. See Chap. IV, *Contemporary Drama of Ireland* (Dublin, Talbot Press, 1918), p. 61.

Cousins' short verse play, *The Sleep of the King* (1902) which was produced in the early days of the Irish Dramatic Movement, also expresses this call of spiritual life in terms of an Irish legend known as 'Connla of the Golden Hair'. The theme of this verse play is about a beautiful fairy maiden who decoyed a king's son to the 'Land of the Ever Young' or the Celtic Elysium. Here the character of the Princess symbolizes the 'invisible presence of beauty' or as Cousins calls her 'beauteous nameless one'. The Fairy Princess casts a spell on Connla, the prince and when Connla wants to know who she is, she replies in a mystical tone :

> I am the beggar one amid the throng
> I am the royal beggar at the door
> Of hushed listening hearts. Among the dew
> At dawn I wander, and at eve I breathe
> On upturned faces round the fires of man.

Connla, the young prince, fell in love with the beautiful fairy maiden who has her 'throne among the ageless stars'. Connla's yearning to possess this mystical beauty is passionately expressed in the following speech :

> O Voice that I have heard among the stars
> O eyes that looked for old mysterious caves !
> O arms that I have felt about the world !

The fairy princess says that she can neither be won by words nor by deeds. Connla then asks more passionately :

> Oh tell me then
> How I may win thee ?

'Follow where I go', replies the Princess and tells Connla to come :

> A little past the beating of the heart
> A little past the finger -tip faith,
> It may be in the murmuring homes of men
> It may be in the solitude of the hills.

Connla's father Conn, the old king, who is afraid of the spell cast on his son by the fairy maiden, invites Coran, a Druid Priest, to break the spell by means of his magical power. But nothing can prevent the prince from obeying the call of the fairy maiden. When his old father asks : 'where thou shalt sit as king' ? Connla replies that he will go to that ideal beauty whose throne shall bear no power - proud king - whose throne is with the everlasting stars.

The play ends with the invisible presence of the fairy princess who takes away the young prince from his old father. Here Cousins is successful in using an Irish legend to objectify his own spiritual and mystic quest. This verse play is an allegory of the call of the spirit to the mortals to liberate themselves from their material prisons. Here the young prince's spontaneous response to the call of the fairy princess reflect the essential Celtic spirit, the spirit of an endless quest after the infinite. Most of the Cousins' poems express this particular vision. The Celtic Revivalist spirit in Cousins is merged with theosophy of India. The Celtic myths and legends offered him abundant potential means for expressing mystical and theosophical ideas.

Cousins' poems "Going Forth of Dana", "The Marriage of Lir" and the verse play "*The Sleep of the King*" form, as he puts it, 'a trilogy', which express in terms of Irish legend a spiritual and mystical vision. He remarks in his 'Preface' to the *Collected Poems* (1940) that this trilogy was an expression of his vision of the emergence of the soul of the universe, the call of spiritual life to the soul, and the culmination of the soul's experience in the union of its outer and inner aspects.[16]

In the poem "The Marriage of Lir and Niav" Cousins sees the Celtic God and Goddess in terms of his theosophical knowledge. Lir is, mythologically, the God of the sea, and Niav is the Aphrodite of Irish myth. Cousins sees their marriage as the divine transaction of unifying the subjective and objective aspects of consciousness.

The poem besides its esoteric import, is rich with description of nature's beauty. For example, his description of the spirit of evening to create the ideal background for Niav to meet his bride :

> But, as upon the breathless hours of eve
> The gentle moon ascends the throne of night,
> And beams white love that wakens soft desire

16. See 'Preface', p. IX.

In waiting hearts, so in that throbbing pause came Niav...[17]

Similarly the description of Niav's beauty in the following lines, shows Cousins' descriptive power :

Clothed white as foam her sea-green girdle hung
Like mermaid weed, and how within her wake
There came the sound and odour of the sea,
The swift and silent stroke of unseen wings,
And little happy cries of mating birds.[18]

Here the poet relates the joyous background of nature to that of the first meeting of Lir and Niav. This method of using nature to convey human emotion is a conspicuous feature of Celtic poetry. Cousins' skill in selecting the natural setting for the description of human emotion is remarkable. The happy cries of mating birds symbolically suggests the forthcoming union of Lir and Niav.

Another of his myth poem, *Etain the Beloved* (1922) which was dismissed by Joyce as 'a table book', is an attempt to read Celtic myth in terms of theosophy. Etain and Midir are the archetypes of an ideal couple in Irish mythology. Etain, the beloved wife of Midir, the Irish God, was driven out of the divine hierarchy and become incarnate in the form of a young girl of great beauty. King Eochiadh, not knowing of her divine origin, wooed her and made her his queen. But Midir followed her. He got back Etain as a stake in a chess game. King Eochiadh wanted to keep Etain by force from Midir but he and his soldiers were frustrated when Etain and Midir disappeared as two white swans flying across the sky. Cousins here used the story to illustrate that true souls of godlike spirits cannot be confined into the material world. This poem also shows the poet's tender feeling for nature. His description of the stirrings of life in creatures at daybreak shows his sensitivity to nature and his powers of feeling and imagination :

Somewhere the snips now tapes his tiny drum;
The moth goes fluttering upwards from the heath;
And where no lightest foot unmarked may come,
The rabbit, tip toe, plies his shiny teeth -

17. *Collected Poems,* p. 43.
18. Ibid.

On luscious herbage; and with strident hum
The yellow bees, blustering from flower to flower,
Scatter from dew - filled cups a sparkling shower.[19]

Cousins has probably shown himself at his best in this fine renderings of his minute and poetical observation of nature. The lyrical charm and concrete imagery of the poem appeal to us even when the esoteric meaning is not clear.

Similar sensuous description of nature is achieved in one of Cousins' love poems called "The Fire of Love, the Wine of Love, and the Wings". This poem should be considered as one of Cousins' best where the poet has attained the height of romantic imagination. Here his minute attention to pictorial details often recalls the poetry of the Pre-Raphaelites. The following lines, for instance, strike us by its dreamy and sensuous suggestiveness :

I would walk by the shore of Loch Lein when the midday spell
Lies flat on the looking glass where the purple peak stands still
on its head,
I will watch where the wild drake rises with quack and splash
From the reedy places that hide the desire of the heart.
And it's not alone I will see when the furzes part,
And your hand in the mine. O wine of my life ! it is not of
these
I will think; for my eyes will be filled with the sally trees
In their young sweet grace, when their limbs in the sunlight
shine
As if they were steeped for an age in enchanted wine.[20]

Here the poet's renderings of the silence of the midday scene which is disturbed by the brake's taking off with quack and splash is remarkable. Cousins reminds us of early Yeats when in this poem, the lover exclaims :

I will row my boat on Muckross lake when the grey of the dove
Comes down on the end of the day, and a quiet like prayer
Grows soft in your eyes, and among your fluttering hair
The red of the sun is mixed with the red of your cheek

19. *Collected Poems*, p. 94.
20. *Collected Poems*, p. 115.

I will row you, O boat of my heart : till our mouths have
forgotten to speak
In the silence of Love, broken only by trout that spring
And are gone, like a fairy's finger that casts a ring...
We shall hold our breath...
For a wild white swan will be leaving the lake for the sky
With the curve of her neck stretched out in a silver spear.[21]

The poem combines the intensity of the poet's love for his beloved and his love for nature. He would hold his breath to see the magnificent beauty of a white swan leaving the lake for the sky. In Irish mythology swans' flight symbolises the achievement of the spirit or the soul's flight. For, Etain and Midir, the Celtic Goddess and God, changed themselves into wild white swan and assume thus spiritual life. The Irish believed that in order to enjoy highest ecstasy of love they fly round the ring of heavens through dusks and dawns. The poet and his beloved here wish to be transformed into swans to fly across the sky because they realise that their love on the physical level is a 'poor thing to be bound to four walls'. The lover exclaims :

Oh ! better than these is a dream in the night, our hearts' mute
prayer
That O, Donoghe, the enchanted man,
Should pass between water and air
And say : I will change them each to a wild white swan,
Like the Lovers Angus and Midir, and their loved ones Caer an
Etain.
Because they have loved for love only,
And have searched through the shadows of things
For the Heart of all hearts, through the fire of love,
and the wine of love, and the wings.[22]

That Cousins' lovers and beloved are distinct from ordinary ones is embodied in their longing to 'search through the shadows of things' as Angus and Caer or Etain and Midir have been doing throughout the ages. They want to rise from physical passion to spiritual fulfilment.

---

21. *Collected Poems,* pp. 115-116.
22. *Collected Poems,* p. 117.

Most of Cousins' love poems are romantic and mystical; it is a love for something that is beyond the sphere of our sorrowful reality. This poem is a typically Celtic-twilight poem. The cadence and assonances effectively contribute to the making of sound and sense. The landscape is Irish countryside, heath and lake. The poem has a languid sensitivity and embodies a mystical affirmation through love. Most of his love poems have this nostalgic and autumnal longing in this soft rhythms. The poem has achieved an intensity by combing the poet's philosophy of love against the background of a vivid Irish landscape.

Cousins' attitude to love is theosophical. The dark passion of man's private experience of love is never celebrated in Cousins' love poems. Love as it is portrayed there, is more a soul's emotion which 'has cancelled all the sum/Of all life's lesser loves'. In a poem called "Love's Infinity" the poet while 'caressing' his beloved questions :

> But now your cheek is warm against my cheek
> And is love satisfied ? Nay! evermore
> Your hands are full of promise, and your eyes
> Gleam with a spirit - light I still must seek
> But never find ;[23]

The poet is ever in quest of this 'Spirit-Light' rather than the passion of the body. In another poem called "Love in the Highest" he embodies the same faith and says that 'clasped hands and clinging kiss is not love but love's pale ritual.'

Like the love poems most of his nature poems are backed by a harmonious philosophy in which God, Man and Nature are interpreted in their integral relationship. He has imbibed from the Romantics as well as from the Theosophists the idea of the communion between nature and man. It is this philosophical foundation of Cousins' love and nature poems that make one feel that his attitude to them is consciously theosophical. In most of these poems on love and nature we note that there is often an overreadiness on the part of the poet to connect the description of every natural phenomenon of external nature with the greater mysteries of life.

---

23. *Collected Poems*, p. 113.

"A Bubble Blower", one of his poems written on Indian life and background, follows the same pattern. The sport of the 'Sunbaked', 'rook-like' South Indian boy's blowing bubbles in the air is captured vividly in the poem. Here the little boy, the poet feels, symbolizes God, the 'Master Blower of Bubbles', who'sat and blew/stars and suns and systems, that glimmered and flew/In bubbles that glinted the rainbow tints'.[24]

The sight leads the poet to observe more philosophically at the end of the poem :

For the bubble itself is nothing
But the blowing of bubbles is all.

What he seeks to suggest is that the whole creation is as illusive as the gorgeous bubbles blown in the air but the force or the power working behind this creation is a higher reality. It is not merely that the little suggests, by imagery of the great. But the great is inherent in the little. To Cousins, therefore, every natural phenomenon is shadowing forth this higher reality. His nature poems like "In praise of Earth", "A Hymn to Hidden Loveliness", "A Song of Stillness" reveal the poet's attempt to realize the essence beyond the physical forms of nature.

It is interesting to note that Cousins, the nature-mystic, finds Indian natural background the most conducive to spiritual realization. the sun-lit Indian landscape fascinated him. He devoted one of his entire volumes of poems to the adoration of the sun which illumines most of the Indian landscapes. The volume he has called *The Sun Songs or the Surya Gita* (1922). The book is dedicated to Rabindranath Tagore. Cousins' last poetical work was also called quite significantly, *Reflection before Sunset* (1946). At the sight of the splendour of the snowy mountain, the Himalayas, bathed on the light of the morning sun, the poet exclaims :

Look up ! see tipped with rose,
White on the sky's blue lake, the vast
Himalayan lotus blows ![25]

The sunrise of the Himalayas described in such sensitive terms captures the spirit of classical Sanskrit poetry. The freshness of the

---

24. *Ibid.*, p. 144.
25. *Collected Poems*, p. 302.

morning sun stirred the poet's 'wakening soul' and led him "To something higher than your height/And purer than your snows". What is striking in this poem is the poet's adoration of the Himalayas in a true Hindu religious spirit. The title "Morning Worship" adequately expresses the poet's temper. The imagery of the rising sun which like a lotus blossoming in the blue lake of the Himalayan sky is in the Eastern tradition. The poet's passionate adoration of the Himalayas is expressed in another poem called "The Burden of Immensity". The sublime beauty of the Himalayas with its vastness serves as a more meaningful scripture to the poet. He says that it has enough potentiality to baffle our senses :

On those colossal steeps on life - print stays ;
While death stupendous deeps with Silence fills;
....
Oh ! though the brow with eager search be flushed,
It quails at scripture writ toȯ large to see.
By frigid power my votive hymn is hushed ;
My tribute candle gutters uselessly;
And all my purpose is a petal crushed
Beneath the burden of Immensity ![26]

The spiritual impact of the sublime and super sensuous beauty of the Himalayas hushed the votive hymn of the poet as it does to a mystic who eventually bends in adoration. The sensuous beauty of the Himalayan valley is irresistible for the poet. He says:

O comprehensible dear transient things !
Beauty between a butterfly's frail wings
A dew-edged leaf, the bulbul's golden song

The perception of their transient beauty is leading him to the contemplation of eternity. He exclaims :

To you and to all finite things belong
God's touch familiar on our quivering strings
That to the exiled soul nostalgia brings.[27]

As a theosophist by conviction the poet considers himself an 'exiled soul' who becomes nostalgic at the sight of God's grandeur

26. Ibid. p. 303.
27. *Collected Poems*, p. 303.

scattered in the Himalayan valley. In such poems the Celtic and the Indian imagination meet. Like a pilgrim Cousin wandered almost all over the lower Himalayas. He was not only fascinated by the beauty and grandeur of the natural background but by the beauty and sanctity of the Buddhist temples as well. Most of his poems in the *Tibetan Banners* (1926) are devoted to the description of the Buddhist monks and their shrines. They also reflect his theosophical involvement with Tibetan religion which began with Madam Blavatsky.

Cousins' poems on Indian life and background are of considerable interest. These poems show his sensitivity to Indian landscapes and his love for India which he made his 'spiritual home'. Among all these poems "Offertory in Hindu Manner" and "Unity" deserve special mention for their adequate expression of the essential spirit of Indian culture.

"The Offertory in Hindu Manner" presents a sensitive picture of a Hindu woman presumably of working class and low caste, who goes to a wayside temples to offer her worship. It is the simplicity of her worship that strikes the poet. Unlike others who worship with pomp and splendour, this poor woman from her 'shari's fold' put up Jasmine flowers and rice on the threshold of the temple :

> Then stood she, very calm
> Empty handed palm to palm
> At her naked breast
> Closely pressed[28]

This poem ends with the description of spiritual calm, the woman seems to have attained through her worship :

> The woman wakened from her trance
> Gave a glance
> Up and down the Adyar Road
> Lifted to her head her load;
> Fresh as dew washed day
> Went her way
> Bearing in her heart a bliss
> Drawn from a deeper life than this

---

28. *Collected Poems*, p. 268.

It may be relevant to note in this connection that Cousins was one of the exponents of the 'Temple Entry Movement' in South India and the poem shows his deep sympathy for the low caste women who are not given access to precincts of the temples by the landlords. The poem also shows Cousins' mystic bent of mind admiring the simplicity of worship.

Another poem called "Unity" is an attempt to capture the religious tradition of India. It is striking that Cousins did not write any poems on the poverty and destitution of the Indian people which often stimulate a foreigners' pen and brush. It seems that Cousins is more interested in the spiritual and religious life of the Indian people than the problem and complexity of their secular life. The poem "Unity" tells us the peaceful co-existence of various faiths in Indian soil. It begins with the portrait of the Muslim devotees on their prayer :

> In robe and turban many hued
> They bloom upon the mind,
> A bank of flowers in prayerful mood
> Bending before a wind.

This is followed by the description of Hindu devotees :

> Beside the white towered shrine
> God Shiva's ancient seat
> Field blossoms in the sunlight
> About my wandering feet

The imagery of 'the bank of flowers' and the 'field blossoms' succeed in bringing out the holiness of the scene. The wandering poet who calls himself a 'pilgrim' is inspired by the holiness of the scene. He exclaims :

> In such clear glimpses of the whole
> Our foolish barrier fall;
> For who finds kinship with the soul
> Is kindred unto all.

The Muslim and the Hindu devotees both are in their prayer seek to find unity with the Whole - the universal spirit of God and all men irrespective of caste and creed are contained in the whole. So all barriers dividing human beings fall.

To capture this 'glimpses of the whole' and to realize the kinship of man with God inspired Cousins' poetic practice. As a pilgrims' harp his poetry sings the divine glory underlying the creation. His is always the poetry of adoration and affirmation. That is why, he never writes any satiric or humorous poetry. Light-heartedness of modern poetry is conspicuously absent in Cousins. The fundamental characteristic of Cousins' poetry are its spirituality and affirmation. His poems do not reflect disappointment and despair, anguish and isolation of life. Most of his poems are poems of faith. Addressing some of his contemporaries in a poem called "Rejoinder, To Certain pessimistic Poets" Cousins characteristically says :

Sing, if you must, of death and doom, for me
Waits patient peace beyond men's foolish wars.
Past your lamented autumn I can see
Spring beyond spring through countless calendars :
And hear, past, conquered flesh, the victory
Of the invisible spirits' battle-cars.[29]

Cousins' poetry seeks to embody this victory of man's spirit. He claims that he would always 'play the springs incorrigible optimist' affirming 'man's proud adventurings' and the joy of life.

We never come across in his poems his inner disquiet. The bitterness which overtook most of his generation is transformed into faith in Cousins. He is never concerned with 'Life's futilities' and does not find 'a grim pleasure in growling at the tooth of time and disease with Jeremiahn Joy'. His note of assertion is eloquently expressed when he exclaims :

(You) chant of things that cloy
What dies and what has died
While I condemned to sing
What knows no perishing
The winging not the wing
Monotonously go
My spirit's way

---

29. *Reflection before sunset poems* (Kalakshetra, Madras, 1946), p. 17. cf. 'The winged chariot draining near' of Andrew Marvell.

It is this zeal for singing the immortality of creation and of the human spirit that we often note in the poems of AE. Both of these poets are determined to brush aside the doubts of their time with their strong notes of hopes and affirmation. Cousins says :

Well let who will employ
Their strings in praise of pain;
A jongleur, I of joy,
I seek another strain.

The language and style of these poems reveal the honesty and intensity of the poet's faith. He sincerely believes like the seers of the *Upanishads* that it is joy and not pain which is the truth of life and creation. The genuineness of his feelings and intensity of his faith that ring through the following lines could never be doubted :

Then wherefore should I make
The shrill complaint of sea birds in the dark ?
Nay but as shadows deepen I would play
The spring's incorrigible Optimist.

Cousins' positive contribution to modern poetry is this note of affirmation and optimism. He displays a defiant spirit against life's negation and upholds a faith in the regeneration of man and society.

Harold Monro in his book called *Some Contemporary Poets* (London, 1920, p. 186) mentions Cousins and the poets of the AE group and observes that the salient characteristics of these younger poets of the Irish Literary Revival is their 'religiousness'. Austin Clarke, a modern Irish poet and critic, in his book *The Celtic Twilight and the Nineties*[30] noted the mystical and theosophical trend in the 'younger Irish followers of this School' who, he claimed, 'were theosophists... and were more influenced by AE than by Yeats'. This is also the opinion of the modern critic, David Perkins, who says that most of these poets of the Irish Literary Revival 'were Protestant, and if mystical, theosophical'. We may summarise our estimate of Cousins as a poet with the following remarks of Perkins:

30. See Chap. 'The Celtic Twilight in *The Celtic Twilight and the Nineties* (Dolmen Press, Dublin, 1969), p. 44.

The Genteel tradition was represented in Ireland by James H. Cousins (1873-1956), a poet of Post Tennysonian, cautiously Pre-Raphaelite and ninetyish style, who specialized in Sonnets and mythological tales using Irish mythology.[31]

II

Cousins' interest in drama, as in all the arts, was primarily spiritual. Though like most poets of his time, he found himself drawn into the Irish Dramatic Movement and contributed two one-act plays to the early days of this movement, his genius is more lyrical than dramatic. In our study of his poems we have noted that he is not capable of the complex texture of dramatic poetry. In one of his autobiographical essays, 'Some unrecognised Forces in Poetical Creation' (1941), Cousins admitted that he left drama to others who were better fitted than him to raise a national theatre of his country.[32] This confession of Cousins justifies Yeats' dismissal of him as a playwrights.

His two one-act plays, *The Sleep of the King* and *The Racing Lug* both were written and staged in 1902. They are not powerful plays yet they are considered as significant contributions to the early days of the dramatic movement in Ireland when Irish plays written by the Irish Playwrights were considerably few. On 29 October, 1902 *The Sleep of the King* was performed by the group, Fay's who were well known among amateur companies. The play was however too thin for a theatre and consisted of four characters who seem to typify ideas and emotions rather than living human beings. As we have already discussed this short verse play in our study of Cousins' poetry, we will not go into details here.

All the characters in the play speak with similar cadences - it is the atmosphere of dreaming meditation rather than of action, which is sustained in the play. It is essentially a poem in dialogue and appeals more to the imagination than to our sense of recognition of actual everyday things of life. Connla, the central character in the play, yearns to escape from the world of mundane reality into the world of the Immortals to which he was decoyed by

31. Chap. 'The Irish Scene' *A History of Modern Poetry* (1976), p. 257.
32. See Chap. II *The Faith of the Artist (Essays),* Adyar, Madras, India, 1941, p. 13.

the fairy Princess. This play seems an imitation of Yeats' earlier poetic drama *The Land of Heart's Desire* (1894) which reflects a similar nostalgia for the dream world.

His second play *The Racing Lug* is altogether different from *The Sleep of the King* in tone and temper. It is written in prose and is more realistic. It is set in a fisherman's village on the north-west coast of Ireland. The play opens with the realistic portrait of the fisherman's cottage where an old fisherman Johny is dozing in an arm chair and his wife Nancy and daughter Bell are busy in the kitchen. The quiet atmosphere of the scene is soon upset by the sudden arrival of young fisherman Rob who frequents this house seeking the love of Bell. Rob often accompanies Johny along with other comrades to the sea catching fish. He has come to insist on Johny to go to the sea that evening. He says :

We're thinking of going off to try a haul.
The money we have earned for a month
Past won't burn a hole in our pockets

He further tells Johny that the wind had dropped and crews are ready, awaiting Johny. Johny, who had a fair knowledge of weather, dissuades Rob to make this mad venture during the dreadful time of March when Gales are quite frequent.

Rob knows the tricks of exciting Johny and calls him a 'coward'. Johny, a typically 'moody' and 'selfwilled' Irish man, springs up at once and joins the voyage without caring to say even a goodnight to his wife and daughter, Nancy and Bell.

Nancy, a weakminded superstitious woman, grows apprehensive and her fears have come true at the end of the play. The big boat of Johny and Rob called the 'Racing Lug' has failed to steer through the tumultuousness of the sea during the gales of March, and their boat capsized. All the fishermen were drowned except Rob. Three days after the catastrophe when Rob reaches Johny's cottage, he finds Nancy dead out of heart failure. On the day of catastrophe Nancy dreamt an evil dream seeing her husband was drowned with all his comrades.

But the play does not end with the gloom of death. The local priest or the Minister announces Bell's marriage with Rob who holds himself responsible for her parents' death. The Minister's last words well express the dramatists' point of view :

> The Gales of March blow some to death and some bear safely on to April with its marriage feast of tears and joy; ... His great will be done.

The Racing Lug (1902) is the first play dealing with the sufferings of the fishermen of Ireland. It was Synge's *Riders to the Sea* (1905) that later became a classic example of play on this theme. The accidental similarity between the two is interesting. Both are dealing with the death and anxiety that loom large over the lives of the fishermen of Ireland. Nancy and Maurya both are superstitious and had a premonition of death. In the *Riders to the Sea* Maurya opposes Bartley's going out and in the *Racing Lug* Nancy does the same to her husband. But Nancy could be differentiated from Synge's Maurya who survives successive deaths in her family maintaining a stoical fortitude.

Cousins' play is incapable of reaching the tragic grandeur of Synge's *Riders to the Sea*. In Synge the conflict between man's life and the invisible forces is powerfully captured. *The Racing Lug* in comparison to Synge's play is a minor work and does not succeed in portraying the tragic situation of a fisherman's life.

Yet Cousins should be credited for introducing a subject which found its majestic expression in Synge's *Riders to the Sea* (1905). The situations in both the plays of Cousins and Synge are the same and there is an attempt for the first time in Cousins to portray the character and situation of the fisherman's life of the Northern Irish. Cousins had some first hand knowledge and acquaintance with their life. One can therefore assume that Synge knew Cousins' play as Cousins knew Synge's and he was very critical of Synge's irresponsible exposure of the Irish reality. The shallowness of the closure of Cousins' play depends on the Celtic revivalistic desire to glorify Irish life. Whereas Synge wanted to call a spade and saw into the horror of Irish life. So the difference between the two plays is ideological.

Amongst other plays of Cousins, *The King's Wife* (1919) deserves to be mentioned. It is a poetic drama in four acts and is based on the life of Queen Mira, a medieval Indian legendary figure - whose devotion to Lord Krishna and her mystical songs made her immortal in Indian literature and thought. We have mentioned earlier that Cousins was quite impressed by the devotional school of poetry in India and he rendered some of Mira's songs from Hindi into English. It is his interest in the mystical songs of Mirabai that inspired Cousins to write this verse play on her life.

The play, as Cousins claims, is an attempt to convey 'three types of religious attitudes - the spiritual adventure and breadth of vision of Akbor, the simple devotion of Mira, and the zealous orthodoxy of Rana Kumbha.[33] What he wants to suggest is that Mirabai, Rana Kumbha, Akbor, and his great court poet Tansen, each represented a common Indian aspiration towards the divine life; they hold, as Cousins put it, the promise of a spiritual and aesthetical unification of all communities. The play attains its significance as it was written in a period when unity of India was first threatened by Hindu-Muslim riots.

The play opens with the journey of Akbor and Tansen towards the temple of Krishna at 'Chittore Garh' (Fort) where both being disguised could see Mira and listen to her songs. Akbor whose eclecticism led him to work for the essential unity of all religions, felt inspired to come and see the Queen Mira. Rana Kumbha, the husband of Mira, who is foil to Akbor, is an orthodox Hindu king who 'would rather die/Than let pollution from an alien glance'. The Mughal emperor's visit to Mira, he considers, caused a 'Subtle poison pass into the blood of their untainted race'. On the other hand Akbor is portrayed as a mystic in quest of a spiritual unity of all men. After listening to Mira's songs of the unity of Lord's creation he exclaims :

> ... a door
> Has opened. In the darkness all disguise
> Falls from the soul, and that great liar, sight,
> Is silenced. Those who look shall never see
> Beyond the eyes horizon.[34]

So the division we see is only an illusion of the limited human vision. Responding ecstatically to Mira's songs Akbor says that the

---

33. See 'Preface', p. IV.
34. See *The Hound of Uladh* (Anthology of plays), Adyar, Madras, India, 1942, p. 21.

truth which he seeks to realize has grown as simple as a blade of grass. He says, 'so much her song has taught me'. In his ecstasy Akbor pays his homage to Mira presenting her a necklace under the cover of his offering of flowers which was discovered later by Mira.

The climax of the play occurs when Rana Kumbha calls the court Jeweller to trace out the exact nature of the necklace. The Jeweller explains that it carries the mark of Mughal Emperor who has come stealthily to meet Queen Mira in the temple. The Rana's suspicion is deepnded when he finds his queen holding 'hushed talks with one unseen'. He is quite sure that Mira has broken the marriage vow. He calls at once a meeting of the court and sentences Mira to death on the charge that she has brought dishonour on his lineage.

The play ends with Mira's drowning in the river. When she goes out of the palace at night she meets a beggar asking her : 'where have you come from?' Mira replies in a mystic vein :

We are not the wind
That it should matter where we have come from
We are immortal flames, and where we go
Is all the matters.

The beggar asks again, 'where are you going ?' Mira answers 'where but to holy Brindaban'. The beggar is confused and warns her that she cannot reach Brindaban by that road which is leading to the turbulent river. Mira's answer again comes with a mystical ring :

Have you never heard
Of the Brindaban built within the heart
That one may reach through water or through flames ?

This is one of Cousins' basic themes that the kingdom of God is within us. Finally Mira gets herself drowned into the river in darkness and triumphs over the jealous orthodoxy of her husband.

Here Cousins is capable of creating an atmosphere relevant to the character and action in the play. The character of Akbor and Kumbha are admirably drawn. Cousins' theosophical mind appreciated Akbor's attempt to establish a synthesis of religion called *Din Ilahi* which was based on the idea of universal brotherhood of man. Cousins' Akbor is not an emperor but an explorer of spiritual truth. The language he speaks is the language of a poet or a philosopher. Whereas Rana Kumbha speaks in prosaic terms. The following speech of the Rana distinctively reflects his character :

> My business is with stern and present thing
> Not with pale phantoms and vague prophecy.

Kumbha presents the crude matter-of-factness of a tyrant who disbelieves in the claims of the mystic. His excessive pride in his sacred Rajput Hindu lineage turns him mad and he fails to realize the goodness and loyalty of his queen. The play wants to show the victory of the spirit of Mira that she, in the intensity of her faith sought death to record her triumph. She knows that through death she finds the holy spirit of Krishna in life. The play is essentially a spiritual play and is one of the finest achievements of Cousins' interpretation of the fundamental religious spirit of India.

CHAPTER - V

COUSINS AS A LITERARY CRITIC AND AN AESTHETICIAN

In our earlier chapter we have seen Cousins as a poet and playwright who sought to combine Celtic imagination with theosophical wisdom in an inclusive vision, or synthesis. He has attempted a similar synthesis in most of his critical and aesthetical writings as well.

We have already mentioned that the Theosophical Movement ushered in a new spiritual enthusiasm in Ireland during the last decade of the nineteenth century. Most of the nationalists and writers of the Irish Revival who were directly or indirectly influenced by the Theosophical Movement believed in Madam Blavatsky's claim in 1888 that the first Kali Yuga or Iron age would come to an end in about nine years and that a great prophecy of the dawning of a new age would be fulfilled.[1] In her book, *Key to Theosophy* (1889), Blavatsky similarly announces towards the close of the century "you will invariably find that an outpouring or upheaval of spirituality, or, call it mysticism, if you prefer" would prevail.[2] Emphasizing the Psychic and spiritual change of human mind at the age of transition, she observed that humanity is entering into a new phase of development and the spirit of man is at last awakened.[3]

Yeats and AE both shared the hope of this dawning of a spiritual age. In February 1896 AE had argued that the Sun's passage from Pisces to Acquarius in a few years time would mark

1. Summerfield: *That Myriad Minded Man: A Biography of G.W. Russell - AE*, Colin Smythe, Great Britain, 1975, p. 74.
2. Blavatsky : *The Key to Theosophy*, London, T.P.H., 1889, p. 194.
3. See Blavatsky's Essay, "Tidal Wave", *Lucifer*, Vol. V, 1889, reprinted in *Adyar Library Bulletin*, 1942, 'Blavatsky Number'.

the transition from a Phallic to a spiritual age.[4] In 1900 Yeats declared that "most of us who are writing books in Ireland today have some kind of spiritual Philosophy".[5] This spiritual revival which Cousins anticipated like his two elder compatriots, coloured his understanding of the new trends of modern English literature.

In fact, Cousins' first and foremost critical work, *New Ways in English Literature* (1917) was written during this transitional period and was marked by new hopes and aspirations. This was a pan-European Phenomenon. Writing about this change in the intellectual and spiritual outlook of the generations before the First World War Jacques Riviere, a French Critic, observed that "a sharp little wind is being blown suddenly through the darkness and boredom of the dying Nineteenth Century. Once more it is morning. Everything is beginning again".[6] Cousins fully shared this faith.

It is this hope for a spiritual change which was also noticed by Virginia Woolf. In response to the first exhibition of Post Impressionistic Paintings which was held in London in 1910, she remarked that the new paintings is a witness to the fact that human consciousness has changed. In this same year the Russian artist Wassily Kandinsky, often called the founder of Abstract Expressionism, who was deeply influenced by Theosophy, brought out his 'epoch making' book *Concerning the spiritual in Art* (1910).[7] Through this book he worked out a combination of mysticism and aesthetic doctrines envisaging a new kind of art that would solve the problems of the spirit by embodying inner experiences of man.

Cousins' book *New Ways in English Literature* bears all these characteristics of the age and his critical outlook is based on a Theosophical belief that the thought-life of humanity is constantly developing and renewing itself. He claims that the literature produced by some writers of this transitional age is contributing to this spiritual resurgence. He observes that the longing reflected through the works of various poets are a testimony to "man's inward

---

4. *That Myriad Minded Man*, p. 76.
5. 'The Way of Wisdom', *The Speaker*, April, 14, 1900, p. 40.
6. Robson : *Modern English Literature* (1970), O.U.P., p. xiv.
7. Campbell : Chap. 'The influence of Theosophy East and West', *Ancient Wisdom Revived* (1980), p. 169.

thirst for a deeper, more lasting reality which may be termed as Spiritual."[8]

In the 'Preface' of the book he has made his affirmation quite clear saying that the change of human consciousness which has dawned on humanity in this age, would definitely affect the literature of the twentieth century. He says:

> Certain it is that the larger knowledge and experience that have been important characteristics of life, West and East, during the past thirty years, are bound to affect profoundly the literature and criticism of the future (p. xiii).

What he has meant by the phrase "larger knowledge and experience" becomes quite clear, when he says that, genuine poets cannot escape from the "two major discoveries of the age and place - the fact of the survival of death by the human consciousness, and the inference of the fundamental unity of all mental life in a supermental consciousness" (p. 10). What is evident here is Cousins' special interest in those writers who reflected in their works a faith in the immortality of human consciousness and the fundamental unity between humanity and divinity.

So Cousins starts with a thesis and unlike other literary historians and critics he wants to be selective. He seeks to make a survey of the development of modern English literature from the perspective of the evolution of human consciousness, indicating the landmarks of the growth of spiritual outlook in literature. His poets may not necessarily belong to the same period in his survey but he felt that "a definite consciousness of purpose revealing itself through the divergencies of these poets" could be chalked out.

In the *New Ways in English Literature* Cousins intends to describe the trends of development in English literature of the late nineteenth and early 20th centuries. Yet he does not hesitate to include here mid-nineteenth century American Poet Emerson, whom he considers one of the forerunners of the "Spiritual trend" in English Poetry. The Irish Poets, particularly Yeats and AE, and the Indian Poet Tagore, who became a rage in Europe in the pre-war period through his *Gitanjali*, represented, Cousins felt, the

---

8. 'Preface', *New Ways in English Literature*.

beginning of a new spiritual resurgence in English Poetry. This new spiritual trend was aided, Cousins maintained, by some late Victorian poets like Meredith, Stephen Phillips and Edward Carpenter who are "living links with the past"; he thought that this new trend also reflected in some poets of the Georgian anthologies (1912-22).

That Cousins was chiefly concerned in drawing attention to the new "Spiritual trend" in English poetry, is evident in his evaluation of Tagore. He says: "In reading a new poet, I instinctively search for his greatest word". By this 'greatest word' he means the 'message' or 'Philosophy' which according to him constitutes the vital essence of poetry. He says :

> Tagore's greatest thought is, I believe, his enunciation of the fundamental perfection within all things....the visible creation is not merely symbolised as, but actually is, the Body of God. The Poet, therefore, always sees the Divine working through the human (p. 23).

Cousins presents Yeats, AE, Tagore and Sri Aurobindo as the Poets of the spiritual vision. He says that "there is an affinity in them which is deeper than emotion or thought, and can only be signified by the term spiritual". In dealing with these poets he feels more at ease; the establishment of the 'spiritual affinity' between the Irish and the Indian Poets, was a subject of his life - long interest.

His study of Yeats ("Yeats, the Occultist") in this book is based on his theosophical knowledge and experience. But this study of Yeats is not as impressive as his study of AE whom he called 'the poet of the spirit'. Cousins' response to Yeats is limited but to AE it is total. In the former he keeps himself limited to the Yeats of the earlier phase emphasizing his "immense knowledge of the whole range of occultism" and his intimate association with the Dublin Theosophical Lodge and the Golden Dawn. Writing about Yeats' Occultism Cousins says that some of Yeats' poems :

> disclose him as Occultist in his knowledge of the finer forces and entities of nature, and as mystic in his interpretation of himself and the universe (p. 36).

About an earlier poem of Yeats called "The man who Dreamed of Fairy Land", Cousins observes that it "is a beautiful rendering of the first stages of life after death" and on "The old Age of Queen Maeve", he comments that it "tells of a Great One speaking through a king in trance." Cousins writes of Yeats thus:

> It is this widening of knowledge and deepening of thought that sent Yeats far beyond the Davis era of Irish poetry. His acquaintance with the founder of the Theosophical movement could not but make a profound impression on one whose natural bent towards the occult was reinforced by the knowledge and tradition of his race (pp. 36-37).

Yeats' bent towards the occult was strengthened by his knowledge of Theosophical literature. Cousins thought that Yeats and AE through their knowledge of the occult, would bring about a new force in Irish Poetry and take literature beyond the Davis era. His essay on AE, is a pioneering study of the Irish seer-poet.[9] Here he has called AE 'the most purely spiritual poet in the English language until the advent of Tagore' (p. 47).

Cousins' study of Tagore and Sri Aurobindo in this book deserve special mention. They are treated quite seriously and are compared with the metaphysical poets of English literature. "Tagore's affinities in English literature", Cousins says, "are Herbert, Vaughn and Crashaw, and among living poets, the seer singer of the Irish Renaissance, AE". What appealed to Cousins most in Tagore's poetry is its "interrelatedness of the sensuous imagery with the great facts and intuitions of life". It is the union of sensuous imagery and deep spiritual apprehension of life that Yeats admired most in Tagore's *Gitanjali*. The book appeared to Cousins as the epitome of synthetic vision of poetry, the ideal he found lacking in the European tradition of the Post-Renaissance period. Cousins cherished a similar ideal of bringing together the natural and the spiritual world in his theory of literature and aesthetics. He shared with Tagore the mode of mystic vision and came to claim it as firm basis of his aesthetic quest.

---

9. Cousins' study of AE in the *New Ways in English Literature* inspired an Indian scholar to write a comparative study of Yeats, AE and Tagore - see Abinas Bose : *Mysticism in the Poetry of Yeats, AE and Tagore* (1945). Cousins wrote an 'Introduction' to this book.

Cousins' criticism of Tagore's *Gitanjali* reveals his critical insight :

> *Gitanjali*... has taken its place alongside *The Rubaiyat of Omar Khayyam* as one of the inescapable things in literary culture. Its sense of freshness and revelation is eternal, because its inspiration is from the eternal rock of the Spirit; it does not ooze through the shifting sands of sensualism, or mere emotion, or blind negation. Literature in general will slowly rise towards its nobility and simplicity. Literary criticism will ultimately realise that like the Cosmic Mind, it holds everything in its grasp, discarding nothing that is worthy in human experience, but dignifying all with the fullness of vision and the true perspective that are the specific gift of India to English literature.[10]

This is a high tribute to Tagore and to the tradition of the Indian spirituality - 'the fullness of vision' is what one can call the inclusive vision - 'discarding nothing', that is, the unity of human experience. This he attributed to Tagore's poetic vision. Cousins' appreciation of Tagore should not be taken merely as a part of the Edwardian enthusiasm for mysticism. He remained a true friend and a genuine admirer of Tagore throughout his life. He agreed with Tagore's biographer Ernest Rhys, who said of the *Gitanjali* that, "it may prove to be the vision of India from which we are yet to get a fresher sense of nature and life.[11] Cousins' belief that Tagore would fulfil what was lacking in the Western intellectual atmosphere of the time was undoubtedly a significant remark and this idea was largely shared by many of Tagore's western admirers during the early part of the century.

Cousins' review of Tagore's aesthetic and philosophical work called *The Creative Unity* in *The Modern Review* (July, 1922, p. 66) reveals similarly his insight into the significance of Tagore's thought. Himself an exponent of synthetic philosophy and aesthetics, Cousins examined the disintegration of modern man in the West. He found Tagore a kindred Spirit and appreciated the

---

10. Chap. 'The Indo-Anglian Poets', *Modern English Poetry* (1921), pp. 123-124.
11. Ernest Rhys : *Rabindranath Tagore : A Biographical Study* (Macmillan, New York, 1915), p. 100.

Poets' "plea for the establishment in human relationship of a unity which, by participating in the Divine function of Creation attains peace and joy".[12]

Cousins Wrote:

> What is vital to the world is not the question of the mechanism of these essays or their connection with former presentations of their substance in their author's books on 'Personality and Nationalism', but the fact that they present adequately and maturely their writers' plea for the establishment in human relationships of a unity which by participating in the Divine function of Creation, attains peace and joy; a 'creative' unity in contradiction to the present world-wide religious, racial and social disunity which, because it is essentially uncreative, and merely productive and destructive, is vowed to spiritual abasement, intellectual poverty and physical misery. Such is in brief, the message of *Creative Unity* and of Tagore to the World.

Examining Tagore's Philosophy of harmony Cousins further says :

> Harmony is the condition in which man's true nature, which is spiritual, finds adequate and appropriate expression, for harmony is the medium whereby personality communicates fully and joyfully with personality and finds the high way and communication with the Divine Personality - which is the truth of existence.

Another of his essay, called "Tagore on Tagore" which he contributed to the book, *Gurudev Tagore* (1946), published by the Tagore Society of Madras, is an interesting exposition of Tagore's thought. Here he analyses the works of Tagore as illustration of what he schematically terms the four purities of Tagore, 'of body, mind, desire and action'. What he seems to say is that Tagore achieved a remarkable synthesis of physical, mental, passionate and active powers in his works and through his life.

Cousins is probably the first European critic to write an appreciative study of Sri Aurobindo's Poetry. He thought :

12. 'Tagore's Message to the World : As Proclaimed in his latest book, *Creative Unity*', *The Modern Review*, July, 1922, pp. 66-67.

> The poetry of Aurobindo is a meeting place of Asiatic universalism and European classicism. It is inspired by the philosophy of the Vedas: it is shaped and atmosphered like Greece, or the Greece that is dimly incarnate in English poetry.[13]

He recognises the 'high thinking quality' of Sri Aurobindo's poetry and has called him a 'Philosopher Poet'; he also finds in Aurobindo's poetry "something of the large quietness of Hugo" (p. 27).

Writing about the difference of Sri Aurobindo from other poets, Cousins says :

> What strikes one most in the poems of Mr. Ghose is the difference between his focal point of poetical vision and that of all but a very small minority of writers of verse in English. Nothing is celebrated by him in song for its own sake. The Poet's eyes perpetually go behind the thing visible to the thing essential, so that symbol and significance are always in a state of interfusion (pp. 27-28).

This attempt to capture the spiritual essence of things visible constitutes Aurobindo's uniqueness for Cousins. Referring to the philosophy underlying Aurobindo's poems, Cousins draws our attention to the poet's presentation of images and symbols in his poems. He says :

> Mr. Ghose is apparently philosopher first, but his poetry is saved from being mere philosophical argumentation in verse by his good taste in image and phrase. When he escapes into pure sight and speech, he gives us a wholly delightful thing like "Revelation" which stands self-existent in its own authenticity and beauty.

Then he quotes the short poem in full :

> Someone leaping from the rocks
> Past me ran with wind-blown locks
> Like a startled bright surmise,
> Visible to mortal eyes, -

---

13. Chap. 'The Philosopher as poet : Aurobindo Ghose', p. 27.

Just a cheek of frightened rose
That with sudden beauty glows,
Just a footstep like the wind
And a hurried glance behind,
And then nothing, - as a thought
Escapes the mind ere it is caught
Someone of the heavenly rout
From behind the veil ran out. (pp. 29-30).

Commenting on the poem Cousins says that such an ethereal unearthly experience of beauty in the abstraction of a thought or 'bright surmise' would perhaps be beyond the powers of response of readers fed on crude realism of the day :

> I would venture to suggest that in letting slip such beings from the unsullied Eden of his genius, Mr. Ghose gives something that will spoil our taste for more concrete and less living work.

Thus Cousins thought the Indian poets are likely to contribute to the growth of new trends in English poetry.

Among English poets Cousins appreciated Meredith's poetry because in it he found a similar remarkable synthesis of abstract and concrete. In the very opening lines of his essay on Meredith,[14] Cousins emphasizes his Celtic heritage saying that because of this he perhaps could touch the deeper and higher regions of the mind as well as the work-a-day level of life in his poetry. Meredith the poet is more important to him than Meredith the novelist. It is poetry, Cousins says, that provides him with a vehicle capable of expressing his deeper spiritual vision. This deeper vision, Cousins finds in Meredith's poem like "The Lark Ascending". The lark which sings 'seraphically' in this poem, represents for Cousins a spiritual voice of the 'Sphere Devas' (p. 95), a theosophical term meaning the realm of the Absolute Beings. He reads in this poem the prophecy of a new era of spiritual resurgence, saying that "we need the lark's unification of joy which is its inevitable expression". In another poem of Meredith, "Hymn to Colour", he finds "a majestic eulogium of the arts as a regenerative power". "Here (Meredith) traces", Cousins says, "with great love, as of a painter,

---

14. Chap. 'Some Characteristics of George Meredith's Poetry', *New Ways in English Literature*.

the miracle of colour in sky and grass, in dew drop and wings" of birds and insects and "to his seeing eye it becomes something more than a matter of pigment : it becomes a finger of God beckoning Humanity onwards, yet not renouncing the world of senses but spiritualizing it" (p. 97). It is this balance of the world of spirit and the world of the senses, the soul and self, that Cousins finds in Meredith's poem, "Outer and Inner". This poem, according to Cousins, shows "the Poet's splendid mastery of details in observation; and his great power in setting them to exquisite music, and lifting the whole to the level of spiritual vision" (p. 99). Cousins appreciated Meredith's joyous acceptance of the idea of the evolution of the spirit, of life as a process of becoming.

Similar attempts of spiritual vision Cousins finds in two excellent narrative poems, "Marpessa" (1890) and "Christ in Hades" (1896) of Stephen Phillips. According to Cousins, the spiritual splendour underlying these poems reflect Stephen Phillips' poetic genius. But his plays like *Herod* (1900) and *Ulysses* (1902), in Cousins' estimation, failed to reveal his true genius. Cousins thinks that Stephen Phillips' fame will ultimately survive on those two narrative poems mentioned above. The suggestion of a spiritual life behind phenomena in these two poems led Cousins to remarks :

> "I have put it down also because of the example that it gives of the literary imagination of the West breaking, by stress and emotion, through the limitation of the single life, and finding rumours and hints of other lives - a matter which will appeal with force to those Indian lovers of literature, who are speaking for the fundamental spiritual unity through which the arts of the East and West will find the way into each others sympathy and understanding" (pp.-66-67).[15]

The spiritual unity of being which is the object of search among both Eastern and Western poets is revealed more emphatically in another contemporary writer Edward Carpenter. "The Supreme purpose of his work", Cousins observes, "is the

15. It is interesting that Cousins' hint was taken by Tagore and he translated or rather adopted the theme of "Marpessa" in his exquisite Bengali poem called "Surdaser Prarthana". See, Pravat Kumar Mukhopadhyay's essay, "Stephen Phillips, and Rabindranath" in a Bengali literary monthly, *Kali O Kalam*, Vol. 4, May, 1971, p. 1149.

mother aim of moulding life beneficently and not life in its forms only, be they ever so admirable, but in its spiritual essence".[16] Cousins finds in Carpenter a strong affirmation of his own faith in the development of a new higher consciousness in humanity. Carpenter's vision sees, Cousins says, "with the evolutionary eye the stupendous process of development along the surface of life, and it sees also with the inner eye the accumulation of faculty and consciousness that lifts thought from degree to degree towards a divine culmination" (p. 91). This echoes Cousins' own theosophical faith in the spiritual evolution of humanity.

Cousins' essay on Carpenter called "A Prophet of Democracy : Edward Carpenter" is partly a biographical sketch and partly a critical study. In fact, the Cousins knew Carpenter personally and were his great admirers. Cousins says : "In Carpenter the claims of modern Feminism in its more spiritual connotation found a natural sympathiser" (p. 76). Cousins also appreciated Carpenter's effort in creating an understanding between East and West. He was undoubtedly influenced by Carpenter's attempt at evolving a philosophy of synthesis of all human thought by examining the findings of Eastern metaphysical thought in the light of western philosophy and science which Carpenter attempted in his work, *The Art of Creation* (1904). It is such a venture that Cousins later made in his aesthetic and philosophical work, *A Study in Synthesis* (1934).

Cousins is one of those critics who responded sympathetically to Carpenter's significant poetical work *Towards Democracy* (1883). Examining his philosophy of democracy Cousins says :

> His democracy can be no little economic formula, no method of "one man one vote", for his vision is towards and that means infinity: the foot of the Imagination is set lightly on the present, but is springing always towards the future. To such a mind there can be no halting-places in systems or creeds....the Higher Democracy of Carpenter which is inspired by the vision of a humanity so purged of self by love that in its units and groups it expresses the abstract beauty and truth, justice and freedom of the spiritual whole (p. 90).

16. 'Chap. A Prophet of Democracy : Edward Carpenter', p. 77.

Cousins found in Carpenter a kindred soul as the English poet insisted on the spiritual wholeness of man envisaging a humanity purged of selfcentred individualism. The realization of the spiritual wholeness of man constitutes the fundamental quest of the theosophists. As a theosophist it was therefore natural for Cousins to feel a spiritual kinship with Carpenter and to interpret his works in terms of Theosophy.[17]

Cousins' short essay, "Emerson, the poet as Philosopher" is also a study of the American poet and thinker from a Theosophist's point of view. Here he looked upon Emerson as the progenitor of a theosophical attitude in the Western literature. Emerson, whom Cousins calls, the harbinger of spiritual resurgence in English poetry, "adopted the point of view now commonly known as theosophical". Explaining this he further remarks :

> The focal point of his inspiration is not in the physical plane, like the modern continental schools before the war; nor in the emotional plane, like the bulk of present day English poetry. It is in the higher mental plane (p. 127).

'The higher mental plane' is a theosophical term used by Blavatsky meaning spiritual consciousness. Like a theosophist Emerson, Cousins argues, "sees one life in all lives, and in all other operations". He sees progress as a movement from gross to fine, from objective to subjective". The poets and writers who embody this spiritual vision in their writings, according to Cousins, are the pioneers of the new ways in English literature.

Cousins, however shows his limitation as a critic in his failure to approach Synge in his essay, "Synge, the Realist on the Stage". This is an entirely unsympathetic criticism and is shorn of all attempts at understanding. It seems that Cousins judges Synge's works from the perspectives of the ideals and aims of the Irish Revivalist Movement and he finds him deficient by the standard of the Manifesto of the Irish Dramatic Movement of 1897 which claims : "We will show that Ireland is not the home of buffonery and

---

17. For Carpenter's influence on the Theosophists see F.L. Woodward : "Walt Whitman, A prophet of the Coming Race", *Theosophical Review*, August, 1903.

easy sentiment.... but of ancient idealism".[18] Cousins seems to be impatient with Synge because he hurts the feelings of the Irish people through his demystification of the Irish peasant life in his plays. In his treatment of Synge Cousins reflects the tone and temper of his time. Himself a Revivalist, he cannot tolerate Synge's destruction of the myth of a 'heroic Ireland'. He finds fault with Synge's notion that the didactic plays of the Revivalists belong to 'the infancy of drama', that maturity must assume writing with aesthetic purpose alone :

> With conscious purpose, Mr. Synge set himself to write *without* purpose, lest his work should be regarded as belonging to the infantile stage of evolution. "The infancy and decay of the drama", he tells us, "tend to be didactic": "the drama, like the symphony, does not teach or prove anything". Apart from the historical and psychological fallacy of these two statements (of Synge), we are left with the implication that it is an offence against manhood for the drama to become tutorial. So be it. But we were in the infancy of Irish drama and some of us claimed the right to be didactic, for the purpose of the time, and Mr. Synge's work, on his own showing, stands as an anachronism (pp. 114-115).

What Cousins wants to suggest here is that Synge's dramas did not serve the nationalist cause for not being didactic. He does not appreciate Synge's negative presentation of the stark reality of Irish life. Drawing our attention to his presentation of "the spectacle of a number of men in the bestial stage of drunkenness retching over the holy stones at the end of a funeral" in a Synge's play Cousins says that here :

> The taste of the realist has gone a step further than that of the normal and real, and has reached the stage when putrefaction is the height of taste, as it is with lovers of game and high cheese (pp. 120-121).

Here Cousins reflects the popular contemporary view of Synge without the critical discrimination of Yeats and Joyce and thus he failed to respond to Synge, the greatest genius of the Irish Theatre.

---

18. *The World of W.B. Yeats*, Ed. Robin Skelton & Ann Saddlemeyer (1965), p. 198.

In spite of its limitations and prejudices of the time that it reflected, *New Ways in English Literature* is interesting as it seeks to mark out a fresh direction in English literature of the first decade of the twentieth century, the so-called 'Edwardian period'. More so, the book gives us a fair indication how some writers of India came to be considered in a big way to have set the tone of literature of the English speaking world. The book is marked with an expectation of something new in English Poetry. The 'Spiritual trend' that Cousins finds in the development of English poetry of the nineteenth and early twentieth century inspired Sri Aurobindo to write essays on poetry, his magnum opus in literary criticism *The Future Poetry*. Sri Aurobindo who was quite impressed by the Critical insights of Cousins, reviewed *New Ways in English Literature*, and said :

> It is not often that literary criticism of the first order is published in India. *New Ways in English Literature* is pre-eminently of this kind.[19]

Sri Aurobindo was struck by the opening chapter of the book where Cousins envisages the symptoms of new development of English literature :

> When in some future volumes from one or other of the new writers of the west we catch the large accent, the forward vision of the self-realised and ecstatic soul, we shall know that the new ways in English literature are breaking through obstructions of ignorance, and that hangs thereon, in the broad highway of literary evolution (p. 15).

This conscious indication of further development of literature in a spiritual line must have inspired Sri Aurobindo with the hope that his philosophy was making a dent on the western mind and he was eager to present his perspective on the development of poetry which resulted in *The Future Poetry*.

Cousins' view of the future mode of man's creative expression is reflected in his essays called "The Future of English Poetry", the tone and the title of which definitely anticipated Sri Aurobindo's group of essays on the future of Poetry. It may be relevant to

---

19. Arya, Vol. 4, 1917, p. 310 - also cited in *The Future Poetry*, 'Introductory', p. 1.

mention in this connection that Edmund Gosse's lecture called "The Future of Poetry" was published in June 1913 by the English Association in Oxford. What I want to suggest by this reference is that a concern about the future growth of English poetry was in the air in the first decade of the twentieth century. Cousins was inspired by this climate of thought of his time, and he transmitted this to Indian scholars and poets. In his essay Cousins puts his perspective of growth clearly :

> The path of progress moves out of the realm of physical and emotional. We are approaching the intellectual; and the spiritual gives hints that some day the general level of poetry will not be far below that of the rare superlative masters in song now, the masters, whose eyes are not dazzled by the surface-glitter off the picture of life, who see through life to its meaning; whose ears hear not only "the still sad music of humanity"; but the deep glad chant of Divinity in humanity; whose thoughts turn ever towards the highest truth and its realisation in life.[20]

Cousins here is applying theosophical philosophy to literary history. In these lines he observes that evolutionary process is entering into an intellectual plane of development affecting all humanity. At this stage the general level of consciousness will rise to the level of the poet of genius whose eyes are not dazzled by the surface glitters off the picture of life and who will see into the deeper springs of life. Cousins envisages that in the writing of these poets concern for humanity will go hand in hand and in this stage of development every one would be conscious of the highest truth, and the mind and heart of man would be transformed. For Cousins this realisation of the transformation of human psyche or mind into a higher level of spiritual dimension will open new ways in English literature. He therefore seeks to adumbrate a view of poetry not unlike that held by the writers of ancient India :

> There may come a time...when the longest poem will be three syllables, the first speaking the Divine Totality, the last speaking the equally Divine fragment of consciousness, the

20. See Chap. 7, *Modern English Poetry : Its Characteristics and Tendencies* (1921), pp. 213-14.

> middle syllable speaking mutual recognition - OM TAT SAT as it is in Sanskrit; the whole looking to its smallest part and singing 'I am That', the part looking towards the whole and singing "That am I" (TAT TVAM ASI).[21]

It is interesting to note that this formulation of poetics based on the tradition of the sage poets of the *Upanishads* inspired Sri Aurobindo to affirm "the mantra of the Real" as the expected course of future poetry. It is not important perhaps who influenced whom but what is worth noting is that Cousins seems to have found a meeting point of the aesthetic principles of Eastern Literature and the current poetic thought in the west.

For him poetry of the future would be synthetic as he insists that synthesis is the fundamental business of poetry. Unlike Eliot, Pound and other modern poets Cousins lay more emphasis on synthetic vision. He prefers the poetry of the achieved vision not the analytic process of vision, the complex delight in the process of exploration which the modern poets seem to prize. Cousins in his 'Preface' to *New Ways in English Literature* has made his objective quite clear when he says that his is a search for a deeper unity in literature that may embrace both idealism and realism. Cousins' ideal poet was AE, the poet of achieved vision.

For this aspiration towards a principle of synthesis or 'a deeper unity' Cousins was inspired by the writings of Emerson, Carpenter, AE and Tagore. It may be mentioned that his book *New Ways in English Literature* carried a dedicatory poem to Tagore where he says :

> Our backs may bend with growing debt
> For your pure golden poesy.

It is this synthetic vision of poetry and philosophy which came to be neglected in English literary tradition of the nineties where, Cousins says :

> A poet is a poet, and a philosopher is a philosopher; and if a poet embarks on the business of philosophy he is frowned upon as if he had outraged some principles of trades unionism.[22]

---

21. 'The Future of English Poetry', *Modern English Poetry*, p. 194.
22. See Chap. 'Literary Ideals', *The Renaissance in India* (1918), p. 161.

Practice in India could therefore be a corrective to the West. This 'dissociation of sensibility' what Cousins is preaching here in a popular mode of language, has been a subject of debate since Eliot talked about it. This separation of sensibility from thought, of poetry from Philosophy was not considered to be an ideal state. Cousins says :

> In India, it appears to me, there has been no such separation made between the various functions of humanity. In the West we have a proverb that you cannot whistle and chew meal; but in the East I have seen a poet whistle a song of the Lord, and at the same time chew the profoundest philosophical concepts with the ease and enjoyment of betel.[23]

Here Cousins suggests that in the Indian mind the mundane and the metaphysical mix very freely and can leap from one to the other casually with the ease of chewing a betel leaf. He draws our attention in this connection to the songs of the bauls, the itinerant minstrels of Bengal, and the songs of Mirabai, Tukaram, Kabir and Tagore which seem to exemplify this mode of synthesis. Cousins says: "India showed me the examples of Mirabai, Tukaram and Rabindranath Tagore, in whom life, religion and Philosophy are one, and sing themselves in the poetry of spiritual joy".[24]

Through his exposition of these Indian poets, Cousins wanted to show the falsity of the assumption that "Philosophy robs poetry of feeling, the one being of the head, the other of the heart". He holds that poetry should express the true relationship of thought and feeling, and their mutual service should be employed in the evocation of deeper nature of one's being. In his books *The Renaissance in India*[25] and in *Samadarsana*[26] Cousins seeks to establish the integral relationship of poetry and philosophy, from the perspective of Indian Psychology and aesthetics.

The fundamental idea of these chapters is that generally in the Western literature, philosophy and poetry, are placed in water tight compartments but there is a fusion of philosophy with poetry, of thought with feeling, of intellect with intuition in the songs of the

---

23. *The Renaissance in India* (1918), p. 164.
24. Ibid.
25. See Chap. 'Philosophy and Poetry' and 'Literary Ideals'.
26. See Chap. 'Samadarsana in Modern Indian Poetry'.

Indian seer-poets. He sums up his observations on this issue saying that, "I cannot resist the temptation in passing to remark that it might be more than fitting if some closer union were established between any system of thought and the eldest of the arts, poetry.[27]

This synthesis of poetry with philosophy has been the subject of debate from Sidney to F.R. Leavis. It is on this issue that Leavis crossed swords with Rene Wellek on the page of *The Scrutiny*.[28] Here Leavis remarks that Philosophy and literature or literary criticism are two different kinds of disciplines. He says that "the reading demanded by poetry is of a different kind from that demanded by philosophy. Philosophy we say, is 'abstract' and poetry 'concrete'. Words in poetry invite us not to think about and judge but to 'feel into or become' - to realize a complex experience that is given in the words".[29]

Cousins' aesthetic quest opposed to what Leavis upholds towards the unity of poetry and philosophy, of abstract and the concrete was primarily a reaction against the trend of the poetry of the nineties. His seems to be a protest against 'Pure Poetry', the slogan of the aesthetes. He hoped that English poetry would be free from its 'narrow rigid and insular' vision if it could assimilate spiritual thought and experience embodied in Celtic Revival and the new poetry of the Indo-Anglian School. This would generate in English poetry an 'inwardness' or 'inlook' as Cousins put it, and an affirmation of the Immanence of the spirit. The important poets who appeared to be the 'forerunners of this new spirit and way of seeing', were already marked by Cousins, Meredith, Stephen Phillips, Carpenter, Yeats and AE.

In the *New Ways in English Literature* references to these modern poets and their other contemporaries, like Rupert Brooke, Masefield, Hardy, De La Mare and D.H. Lawrence occur only incidentally, but Cousins dealt with them in a much broader

27. See Chap. 'Philosophy and Poetry', *The Renaissance in India* (1918), p. 194.
28. See *The Common Pursuit* (Chatto & Windus, London, 1962), Chap. 'Literary Criticism and Philosophy', p. 212.
29. Ibid., p. 212.

perspective in his later critical work, *Modern English Poetry : Its Characteristics and Tendencies* (1921).

This book as Cousins himself admits in the 'Preface' forms an extension of and a sequel to the *New Ways in English Literature*. The book is the result of a series of lectures on Modern English Poetry that he delivered in Keijijuku University, Japan, in 1919 on the strength of which he was conferred the honorary degree of Doctor of Literature. Here Cousins has made a broad survey of modern English poetry in the English Language indicating its 'probable future trends'. Among other things he offered here an important critical and historical insight into the emerging concept of a modern commonwealth literature which has now been accepted widely :

> Till the time of Shakespeare and for some time afterwards, English poetry was the poetry of the English. To-day it is not the poetry of a country but of a language. There are English poets who have never seen England. There are books of English poetry which have never been opened in Fleet Streets (p. 1).

He rapidly glances over the big field - Australia, Canada, America, India and Ireland and points out local variations that have taken place, "the deeper influences that have been exerted on English Poetry through its contact with the spirit of the East and with the Irish spirit" (p. 16). He traces the history of English poetry in the Nineteenth century and so far England is concerned, he takes up four late Victorian poets, Watson, Bridges, Hardy and Carpenter, the last of whom he has already dealt with in the *New Ways in English Literature*.

He considers Bridges as the supreme love poet in modern English poetry. Analysing a series of shorter love lyrics of the poet, he remarks that Bridges has sung of love in every mood and he is primarily a poet of love who "takes his place with honour among the great lovers in song" (p. 37). Cousins reveals his own characteristic preference when he says that Bridges has sung of love "with a purity" and it is free from "the taint of morbid preoccupation with a mere sex function which shows itself as a disease in the poetry of today" (p. 37).

No wonder that he failed to appreciate the love poems and the poems of animal life of Lawrence whom he called "The Laureate of youth's futilities" (p. 59). A transcendentalist in temperament and expectation, Cousins could never be sympathetic to the stark eroticism of contemporary English and American love poetry. He says :

> But in most of the sense-poetry of today, or indeed of any day, we become aware that it is a matter of nerves, not of consciousness. An emotional and neurotic uneasiness is mistaken for the solemn disturbance of the 'Divine Afflatus'; an imflamation, which is of the senses, not an inspiration, which is of the spirit (p. 60).

It is quite clear from this statement that Lawrence's mode of immediacy of perception was too raw for Cousins who is seeking a higher consciousness in English poetry. But his insight is correct - 'the neurotic uneasiness' and a sensitive presentation based on nerve sensations is there in Lawrence's poems - only that in modern context we consider them to be the positive quality of Lawrence's achievement. So in spite of his dismissal of Lawrence, his reading of Lawrence is quite genuine. Settled consciousness - the achieved wisdom is not the subject matter of modern art and poetry but the throbbing process of experience.

This limitation of sympathy in Cousins' critical judgement is also evident in his study of the poetry of Rupert Brooke, who was one of the leading poets of the Georgian School. Of his poetry Cousins says :

> 'It is not always the most beautiful caterpillar that becomes the most beautiful butterfly' - and Brooke, from the point of view of literature, was only a caterpillar; neither can we judge his poetry through his character and his more or less romantic death (p. 56).

This in a way is a more original perception of Cousins - here he refers to Brooke's self conscious realistic poetry. The stark realism of Brooke's poetry does not appeal to Cousins as he is impatient of poetry based on surface realism.

This is why, De La Mare seems to be more interesting to him than Brooke. He appreciates De La Mare's "faculty for bridging the border between waking and dreaming - between reality and fantasy" in his poetry. Appreciating his poetry Cousins observes: "De La Mare's poetry is always a wonderland brought to earth or the earth transfigured wonderland." De La Mare's conviction: "What our senses perceive of the world about us is not all, there is to know" Cousins heartily approves of. He therefore, seems to be less impatient towards De La Mare, Masefield and Hardy whose poetry survey an area of consciousness that runs deeper than the superficial vision of reality. Admiring Masefield and Hardy he says that they "share something of the noble seriousness of great poetry".

Masefield's poetry which has occasional glimpses of the spiritual truth hold out, as Cousins put it, hope for the future. He says, "Masefield stands high, perhaps highest, among his contemporaries by reason of the element of thought and philosophical utterance i.e. in his poetry" (p. 67).

The same note of prophetic vision Cousins finds in Hardy's poetic drama, *The Dynast* which was published in three parts in 1904, 1906 and 1908. What struck him in Hardy is that, he presents the prophetic vision of the spiritual evolution of human consciousness against the backdrop of the great Napoleonic wars. Interpreting the prayer of the Pities in the concluding lines of *The Dynast*, Cousins says :

> This assurance springs radiant and eloquent, out of the last line of *The Dynast* :
>
> But a stirring thrills the air
> Like to sounds of joyance there
> That the rages
> Of the ages
> Shall be cancelled, and deliverance offered from the darts that were,
> Consciousness the Will informing, till it fashion all things fair
>
> (pp. 46-47).

In these lines Cousins finds "that consciousness gradually moving the Will into action will remould this "sorry scheme of things", "nearer to the heart's desire" (p. 47). This hope of an awakened universe to its spiritual self-consciousness was the hope of renewal that Cousins sought to find in new poetry.

The standard of Cousins' criticism of poetry, therefore, is based on the quality of spiritual vision, which would usher in a new development in English Literature. He says, he does not measure the greatness of a poet "by the ordinary standards of form and tone and quantity, intellectual energy, imaginative sweep and suggestiveness" - but by "the standard of spiritual vision". He says, "greatness in poetry can only spring from greatness of consciousness" (p. 67). The fundamental criterion of his aesthetics is this spiritual vision" - "divine urge, the urge that is primarily towards creation and revelation, and only secondarily towards decoration" (p. 31), and the poets who are not amenable to this way of looking at things are not considered by him as worthwhile.

In spite of this limitation of sympathy and onesidedness, we cannot dismiss Cousins' literary views altogether. He has offered us some valuable critical insights in his treatment of the Irish and the Indian poets. The Irish poets are, in many respects similar to the Indo-Anglian poets. In many respects the history of Ireland and that of India are so parallel that one is led to the irresistible conclusion that there must be some more subtle and deeper connection between the two countries. That is why, most of the Celtic Revivalists like Yeats and AE were identifying England as 'citadel' of 'materialism' and Ireland and India as that of 'spiritualism'. Behind the revivalist movement of both these countries, Cousins therefore, found "an urge to spiritual conquest". Writing about the impact of the Irish Revival on English literature he says :

> It's spirit has begun to translate itself into English poetry as a disturbing influence calling humanity away from satisfactions in things seen or felt or heard, to some deeper satisfaction of the soul, some affirmation of the immortal spirit.[30]

He considers that something of the same spirit may be said about the impact of the Indo-Anglian poets of the early decades of the 20th century on English poetry. He remarks in his characteristic style :

---

30. Chap. 'The Field of Modern English Poetry', *Modern English Poetry*, p. 16.

> ... it will be seen that for the invasion of India by the English language, the East has taken a spiritual revenge by invading English poetry (pp. 10-11).

He affirms that the Indo-Anglian poets are capable of expressing their own direct voices through English language. He shows the deftness of Toru Datta in the handling of the English language. She was followed by Sarojini Naidu "who with a somewhat stronger touch has found an audience in England and America and planted the beauty and mystery of India in many hearts and imaginations beyond its coasts". He seems to suggest that these two poetesses are not accidents of history - their entry into English literature is a beginning and a preparation of further changes in the cultural history of England.

In the *New Ways in English Literature* (1917) Cousins dwelt on the individual studies of two other Indo-Anglian poets, Tagore and Sri Aurobindo, and later in the *Renaissance in India* (1918) he wrote on Sarojini Naidu. But in *Modern English Poetry* (1921) he attempted to generalise on the impact of the whole school of English poetry. It may be mentioned that the word "Indo-Anglian" was invented by Cousins in his chapter on these Indian poets writing in English. The chapter is entitled, "The Indo-Anglian Poets" (Chap. V, p. 117) - a word which has now gained a wide currency specially in distinctive opposition to the term 'Ango-Indian' which refers to literature in English by Englishmen who lived in India. Cousins' great contribution in this field is his evaluation of Sri Aurobindo and some other Indian poets as the pioneer of a new world outlook. But there are many Indian writers who in their zeal for glorifying the national heroes fail to accept sober and balanced assessment of Cousins in proper spirit. For instance, Dr. Kotoky in his book, *Indo-English Poetry* (1969), made uncharitable remarks on Cousins. Kotoky refers to Cousins' "occasional intolerance of Indo-English Poetry". He says: "In the case of the English critic, James H. Cousins', criticism is something hasty and intolerant, and sometimes unduly patronising as in the overall tone of his criticism of Sarojini Naidu's poetry". Apparently Kotoky did not take care to find out the credentials of Cousins as a critic, otherwise he would not have called him an English critic. It is of course true that Cousins shows his disapproval of many things in Sarojini's poetry. For instance, he pointed out that being a dedicated champion of Women's liberation movement Sarojini should have reflected a different attitude in her poems on women. But she seemed to him to have glorified the passivity and submissiveness of Indian women. Cousins says that in her "life she is feminist up to a point, but in her poetry she remains incorrigibily feminine".[31]

What shocked Cousins was this contradiction between Sarojini the poet and Sarojini the political and social activist - Sarojini the feminist and Sarojini the feminine poet. Here all one could say that Cousins probably did not understand the spirit of Indian nationalist movement which sought to glorify the national tradition of the country somewhat uncritically in revivalist terms.

But this does not mean that Cousins failed to appreciate Sarojini's poetry. Kotoky seems to have overstated his case when he says that Cousins' criticism of Sarojini's poetry is 'hasty' and 'intolerant'. Cousins' interpretation of Sarojini's poem called "Feast" might have disappointed Kotoky but he overlooked Cousins' perceptive remarks on Sarojini's nature poems where he did not fail to assess rightly Sarojini's genius. He also appreciated Sarojini's poems on Indian life and religion. Commenting on her poem called "June Sunset" Cousins pointed out that "to get the full flavour of the last two lines some acquaintance with Indian atmosphere, with its amazing variety of vivid colour, is necessary". He also says in this connection that "there are many lines of delicate imaginative beauty that must remain unrivalled treasures to readers - unacquainted with the East".

He appreciated Sarojini's poem "Festival of Serpent" because it has given "a series of delicate presentation of the phases of Indian life". In appreciation of nature in a poem called "Leili" Cousins remarks that the poem "takes its place among the fine things in literature".[32] He did not fail to notice that in this poem "the poetess had exalted India to the literary heavens alongside the throne of Diana of the Classics" (p. 134).

He liked these poems of Sarojini as they reflected the genuine religious feeling and insights into Indian philosophy. He considers

31. Chap. 'The Poetry of Sarojini Naidu', *The Renaissance in India*, p. 262.
32. Chap 'Indo-Anglian Poets', *Modern English Poetry*, p. 133.

Sarojini's poem "to a Buddha Seated in a Lotus" a poem of great beauty. It is obvious that Cousins would not have composed a poem on Sarojini Naidu if he did not truly admire her personality and her poetry. He delicately says of the poetess who came to be known as the Nightingale of India :

> Such a wind has moved your wings,
> But that from Life's prison sings;
> Caged familiar of the skies -
> In whose spirit - lighted eyes
> India's wisdom deep and long
> Blossoms lightly into song.[33]

In fact, Sarojini Naidu and the Cousins were great friends. Cousins' wife Mrs. Margaret Cousins, who was one of the founders of the Women's movement in India, was Sarojini's closest ally a co-worker. Both of them worked for the establishment of solidarity of the Indian women with the women organizations all over the world.

It is obvious that James Cousins' contribution as a critic of Indo-Anglian poetry is yet to be acknowledged and properly assessed. The fact that he stimulated Sri Aurobindo to take up literary studies anew is a credit large enough for a special mention. Sri Aurobindo has fully acknowledged his debt to Cousins' book, *New Ways in English Literature*. He says that the book posed before him the question of the future of English poetry and that of the poetry of the world. Sri Aurobindo's book called *The Renaissance in India* was also patterned after Cousins' book of the same title. In this book Sri Aurobindo mentions the circumstantial and spiritual affinity between the Celtic Revival and the Indian awakening.

With such a background of interest in Ireland it is not surprising that Sri Aurobindo found in Cousins a kindred spirit. Cousins' interest in Oriental philosophy and mysticism brought them to a close understanding of each other. Sri Aurobindo commended Cousins' genuineness of Oriental Scholarship in an essay called "A Rationalistic Critic of Indian Culture" (1920). Sri Aurobindo says that for a definite view of Indian culture and civilisation one should turn to those who can speak with some authority. He dismisses the work of many so called authority on

33. *Collected Poems*, p. 201.

Indian thought and religion as basically anti-Indian. But Sri Aurobindo says :

> It matters very little to me what Mr. Archer, Dr. Gough or Sir John Woodroffe's unnamed English Professor may say about Indian philosophy, it is enough for me to know what Emerson or Shopenhauer or Nietzche or what thinkers like Cousins and Schlegel have to say about it.[34]

It is quite clear from this statement that Sri Aurobindo held Cousins in great admiration and did not hesitate to include him among the most celebrated thinkers of the West.

Sri Aurobindo found in Cousins a true friend of India, a person who was able to grasp the soul of Indian culture and who was prepared to help in the process of its resuscitation; secondly what was more appealing to Sri Aurobindo's heart, was Cousins' synthetic approach to philosophy and culture. Cousins appeared to him not only as a powerful writer of 'philosophical and critical insight' but a poet and a visionary. Quite naturally a friendship and philosophical understanding developed between them and Sri Aurobindo was generous enough to own that several of Cousins' book and essay influenced his thought on literature of the West.

This closeness of Cousins to Sri Aurobindo has not been usually noted by Aurobindo scholars in India. Dr. S.K. Prasad, for instance, in his book called *The Literary Criticism of Sri Aurobindo* (1974) ignores Cousins' influence totally and credits Sri Aurobindo "for rightly evaluating Meredith, Stephen Phillips, Carpenter, AE, Yeats and Tagore". He says, "It is significant that among the pioneers of the modern age Sri Aurobindo gives a place of honour to such neglected poets as Stephen Phillips, Carpenter and AE". He praises Sri Aurobindo, for presenting "a new perspective" and says that "it is a perspective which we do not usually get in the books of modern poets". Professor Prasad ignores the simple truth that in this new perspective and critical evaluation of the pioneers of modern poetry Sri Aurobindo was by and large indebted to the critical insights of Cousins' *New Ways in English Literature*. Sri Aurobindo admits that he had lost all connections with English literature after his "departure from England quarter of a century ago" and confesses :

34. *Sri Aurobindo Centenary Volume* XIV, Delux Edition (1971), p. 46.

> I had long heard, standing aloof in giant ignorance, of the great names of Yeats, but with no more than a fragmentary and mostly indirect acquaintance with some of his work; AE only lives for me in Mr. Cousins' pages;[35]

Sri Aurobindo affirms that with Cousins' book a new world was opened before him and exclaimed in joy: "I stand Cortez like on the peak of the large impression created for me by Cousins' book" (p. 5).

It was Cousins again who first wrote of the genius of Sarojini's brother Harindranath Chattopadhyay. What is more Cousins sought to establish a parallel between the nature of influence of the Indo-Anglian poets with that of the poets of the Irish Revival. Cousins pointed out that like Yeats, AE and some other Irish writers imparting a typical Irish flavour to English poetry, Indo-Anglian poets, too have bestowed upon it an oriental quality. Writing about Sri Aurobindo's affinity to AE Cousins says :

> For a comparison to Mr. Ghose's double sightedness, the glimpsing simultaneously of norm and form, we had to pass beyond the confines of Europe, and listen to the spiritual songs of AE. The Irish poet has not the patience and expansiveness of his Aryan brother, but in heart and vision they are kindred.[36]

Cousins was obviously the first critic to have compared so authentically Sri Aurobindo with Western poets. He also pointed out the spiritual affinity that existed between Yeats, Tagore and AE. He remarks that Tagore's influence will be felt all over the West "not simply as a translation; but as a powerful original". He discussed Sri Aurobindo seriously as a poet of equal importance with Tagore and as a spiritual force to be reckoned with in the development of poetry in the English speaking world. He has also discussed authentically the poetry of Rami Reddy, Iqbal and the Sikh mystic poet and writer Puran Singh in his book called *Samadarsana* or *Synthetic Vision* (1925).[37] It was Cousins who first brought these Indian poets to the notice of the Western literary world. Here he says that "these gems of poetry in the mine of India's

35. 'Introductory', *The Future Poetry*, p. 4.
36. *New Ways in English Literature*, p. 28.
37. Chap. 'Samadarsana in Modern Indian Poetry', p. 35.

past....Mirabai, Tukaram and Kabir who sang the inmost of their sweetest way". C.F. Andrews, another savant of modern India and Cousins' contemporary, also draws our attention to this 'Bhakti School of Indian Poetry' and his remarks are quite similar to those of Cousins. Andrews says :

> Eastern and Western conceptions of spiritual life are flowing forward today like two great rivers which come from different sources. We need the poet-thinkers, both in the West and in the East, who may be able to cut new channels from one river of human experience to another. In this way the soil of human life will be enriched and its fertile area enlarged.[38]

Cousins' own life and works were dedicated to this achievement of East-West synthesis. He played a leading role in popularising the devotional poetry of the Indian sage poets. He translated some of these poems into English and advised that there should be a collection of their poems written in different Indian languages and should be rendered into English to make them known all over the world.

This interest in Indian thought constitutes one of the important aspects of Cousins' critical and aesthetical writings. He sought to see the western poets and writers in terms of Indian thought. In his essay called "Substance in Swinburne"[39] Cousins offers a new interpretation of Swinburne who is often underestimated by twentieth century critics. Cousins finds that Swinburne's "Hertha" reflects the "vedic conception of the creative Being" - "the Source and the soul of all manifested life". He says that "five centuries before Christ, the Oriental seers realized the existence of this secret and self-existent power which they call the Mother of the universe of *Jagadamba* the World Mother." Swinburne called "Hertha", Cousins quotes :

> I am that which began
> Out of me the years roll

---

38. 'Swami Rama Tirtha : An Appreciation', *The Visva-Bharati Quarterly*, January, 1929, p. 438.
39. (*Prabuddha Bharata*, Vol. 46, Nov. and Dec. 1941) XLVI, pp. 506-509, 544-552.

Out of me God and man;
I am equal and whole.

Cousins here finds Swinburne's celebration "of the cult of a world-Mother which embodies" the Goddess worship of Hinduism and the veneration of the feminine aspects of the Buddha in China and Japan" (p. 548). "The Goddess that Swinburne has in his imagination", Cousins argues;

> ...is no personification of the Mother Earth, she is, to Swinburne, more primitive than primordial substance. She is that conceivable stage of the Universal life out of which Process emerges...In Upanishadic thought she is called the 'Parabrahma', the Universal Soul beyond manifestation (p. 546).

Affirming the philosophical vision of Swinburne Cousins says that "all through his poems, and characteristically in "Hertha" there is a vision of human possibility, nay of human destiny, that next to Shelley's is the highest in English poetry, and akin to the age-long vision of India (pp. 547-548).

Thus in Cousins' interpretation, 'sensuality', 'paganism' and 'blasphemy' which were the charges usually brought against Swinburne, were refuted. Cousins asserts that Swinburne was neither a Pagan nor an agnostic. He says that "Swinburne's ultimate attitude to the universe was not dualistic but monistic though in some of his poems he remains "halfway between the spiritual affirmation of Shelley and the spiritual negation of James Thompson" (p. 508).

Cousins' evaluation of Swinburne from the perspective of Indian thought is as interesting as his evaluation of Shelley from the same stand point. This he has done in his book called *The Work Promethean* (1933). Here he seeks to provide a new knowledge and perspective on the various contexts of Shelley's achievements. His treatment of Shelley is altogether free from the old Ariel caricature and the new critic type of blind hostilities towards Shelley. He has made it quite clear that beneath the symbolic complexity of Shelley's poetry, there is a solid philosophical and socio-political base.

Though the book is the result of Cousins' teaching of Shelley in India (at Madanapalle Theosophical College, South India), his interest in Shelley is a part of the radical revival of Shelley in the last decade of the nineteenth century.

Cousins with his theosophical background tries to explain Shelley's philosophical poems in terms of theosophy. In the opening chapter of the book he has made an attack on those critics of Shelley who sought to underestimate the spiritual context of Shelley's poetry. Cousins tried to contradict the Arnoldian representation of Shelley as 'an ineffectual angel' and saw in his socialistic orientation a concrete interest in matters of society.

He says that Shelley took up vegetarianism as a protest against the disruption of the unity between the individual and the universal being. Explaining Shelley's quest after this fundamental unity Cousins says :

> Any movement towards fulfilment in life of the vision of the fundamental unity, on which Shelley reared the sky-ascending edifice of his creative imagination, involves drastic readjustments in the relationships not only of human individuals and groups but of humanity and its environment.[40]

Shelley, Cousins says, therefore "made his personal peace with nature by renouncing the blood sacrifice of animals for food".

That Shelley had really made a "drastic readjustment in the relationship of human individuals" is evident, Cousins argues, in his great enthusiasm for Feminism. He says that "there is one special aspect of the work Promethean in life in which Shelley's influence has been, that is, the emancipation of women which would be a more complete embodiment of human unity" (p. 116).

Cousins believes that this attitude to womanhood is better expressed in Shelley's poetic drama *Prometheus Unbound*. He says that Prometheus represents the executive aspect of the soul of humanity, operating in the external world, and Asia the shaping, nourishing and conserving aspect. Prometheus and Asia are one and complementary to each other. They are "the symbolical

40. Chap VI, 'The work Promethean in life, Shelley as Social Reformer', p. 115.

expression in terms of human relationship of the mystery of the cosmic duality in unity, of the two aspects, Life and form, of One Being and One Process". Examining their relationship in terms of Indian thought, he says that "their highest expression is celebrated annually in Vedic India in the marriage of Shiva and Parvati" (p. 27). For Cousins, Asia and Prometheus stand "for fundamental aspects of the Cosmic Being and its reflection in humanity...they are the *atman* and *buddhi* (the essential ego and intuition) of the Orient" (p. 31). The term Cousins here uses, shows that he reads Shelley's drama in terms of Theosophy. His treatment of the myth of Prometheus in Shelley's poetic drama is also inspired by theosophical philosophy. He warns us not to see in the sufferings of Prometheus the vindictiveness of Jupiter - that Jupiter and Prometheus symbolise evil and good which are distinct from one another. He says :

> We have to regard these personifications and happenings as co-operative elements within a single process, animated by a single energy, moving towards a single fulfilment (p. 36).

Probably in theosophical vein Cousins here interprets Shelley's idea that good and evil - both are co-operative elements within the process of creation. The sufferings inflicted on Prometheus, are preparatory for his emancipation, as they draw out and strengthen, Cousins argues, Prometheus' wisdom and compassion (p. 36).

"Shelley's teachings therefore", as Cousins puts it, is that "when man has achieved goodness and happiness, external instruction and rulership will have become unnecessary". Man-Promethean, Cousins says, is not only an anarchist teaching that man is superior to law, but he is also the embodiment of Christ, so Prometheus like Christ represents the spirit of Love. He says emphatically that 'man in the highest Man-Promethean, is governed solely and completely by love and thus he sets himself free from law' (p. 38). Reemphasizing Shelley's gospel of love, Cousins says that it is by means of love that man would be 'Man-Promethean'. He reminds us of the inadequacy of Freudian interpretation of love which limits the 'Grand Passion' to sex. Shelley's love, Cousins observes, should not be confused with sex as it "belonged entirely to the psyche". "Love to Shelley", he says, "is the integrating power in the universe"

(p. 38). He criticizes the critics like Aldous Huxley who interprets Shelley's love in terms of sex and fails to understand Shelley's attitude to love as a unifying spiritual power. Cousins' interpretation of Shelley's idea of love is made interesting by a comparison he has drawn between Shelley and Tagore who are according to Cousins, spiritually kindred souls. Cousins observes :

> The Freedom of love that Shelley dreamed of was freedom for love to find its full expression and voluntarily to seek its affinities; the binding that Rabindranath affirms is the voluntary merging of the self of illuminated human being with others through love. The one dreamed of love attainable; the other affirms love present, and invincible if put into action. The Western poet, from the side of humanity capable of Divinity says "we must be free in order to love"; the Eastern poet, from the side of Divinity in humanity, says, "we must love in order to be free", and affirms the recognition of the essential unity of humanity as the measure and test of all movements that take to themselves the sacred name of freedom.

The spell that the great Eastern mystic poet Tagore exercised on Cousins is quite evident in this comparison. No wonder he accepts Tagore's philosophy of love which emphasizes the voluntary merging of the self with others through love.

The universal love of Shelley which is clearly humanistic in character assumes a spiritual dimension in Cousins' interpretation; he relates it to the Theosophist's view of love which is based on the realization of the fundamental unity between the individual and the universal being. "By Love", Cousins says, "in the language of India, man can free himself from the laws of action or *karma*" (p. 37). That he has seen love in this light of Theosophy becomes more evident when he argues that Shelley has conceived love as "a compassionate power, the power of the liberated mind working in complete unity with the sensitiveness of the purified heart". Shelley's *Prometheus Unbound*, Cousins considers, is an attempt to depict the spiritual liberation of man. He says that "the triumph of the Flamebringer over the forces of Darkness not only released himself from the rock to which he was bound, but released the inner powers of humanity" (p. 40). Cousins shares Shelley's view that these inner powers within man are the true index of man's development. He says the gifts including those of speech, science, sculpture, medicine, music, astronomy and social organization that Prometheus gave man, are not, according to Shelley, final accomplishment of humanity. These are only external capacities by which man has survived. Shelley's ideal for humanity, Cousins puts it, "was not a mere elevation of unregenerate life through accumulation of substance and external capacity, for he believed with the Oriental sage Vasistha that the mere addition of the finite to the finite does not produce the infinite" (p. 35). What Cousins seems to suggest here is that in spite of having those gifts that Prometheus gave to man, man remains unregenerate and the regeneration of man could be achieved only by the realization of the inner powers latent in him. Prometheus Cousins thinks, liberates himself by realizing the powers of wisdom and compassion latent in him; Prometheus stands for him as a symbol of spiritual liberator who encourages the development of their inner powers within man which could lead humanity to the Promethean experience of liberation. That is why, Cousins has called his book, *The Work Promethean*.

In a chapter called "The Theism of Shelley, the Atheist" he makes an attempt to find Shelley's philosophical view of religion. Writing about "the awful shadow of some unseen power" that Shelley describes in his poem "Hymm to Intellectual Beauty" Cousins observes that it is not "a taciturn divinity seated far aloof from mortal concerns. On the contrary, as Shelley sees it, with the same clear vision as that of the seer of India who created the *Gayatri Mantram* which expresses the identity of illumination in the universe and the individual, it is Itself the impulse in mankind to knowledge of Itself; the light in humanity through which humanity recognizes the Light of lights. Its push is felt in all things; but the flash of recognition comes with invitation from the human side".[41]

Cousins finds the fullest expression of Shelley's idea of the supreme power of the universe in his "Adonais" where the poet sings of "the One Spirit's plastic stress" sweeping through every object of the universe. It is this Power which is "sustaining the world from beneath and kindling it above" (p. 53). Shelley's idea of the supreme power sustaining and at the same time transcending the creation, Cousins finds, quite similar to the Indian concept of

41. Chap. 'The Theism of Shelley the Atheist', p. 51.

Brahma. He says, "It is not certain whether Shelley had the Vedic wisdom in mind or not...the numerous references to India in his poems would seem to indicate more than a surface interest" (p. 43). Cousins wanted to affirm that Shelley's knowledge of Indian philosophic thought was important for his poetry. Cousins, of course knew that Shelley read William Jones' works very seriously.

Examining Shelley's *Prometheus Unbound*, "Hymm to Intellectual Beauty", "Alastor", "Adonais" and some of his shorter lyrics like "Mutability" Cousins refutes the charges that were brought against Shelley for his atheism. He relates his philosophical position to that of a monist who considers the ultimate Reality as One and indivisible. The oft quoted line from Shelley's "Adonais" beginning with "The One remains, the many change and pass;" Cousins takes as his basic text. Cousins has also written an interesting chapter on Shelley's aesthetic ideals in this book. He believes like Shelley, that the poet, prophet and the philosopher are one. The faculties like emotion, intuition and cognition as Cousins puts it in his book on aesthetic philosophy, *A Study in Synthesis*, are apparently separate but in art and poetry they are blended into harmony. He finds Shelley's writings are ideal examples of this synthetic mode. The synthesis of this emotive and intellectual faculties is revealed in Shelley's "The Defence of Poetry" which has become a classic in English literary criticism. In this chapter Cousins reinterprets Shelley's ideas of the poets as ethical teachers, poetic imagination as an "imperial faculty, the great instrument of moral good". According to Cousins, Shelley was both a philosopher and poet. He agrees with Shelley that poets "are the mediators between the worlds celestial and terrestrial"; and as such there should not be any dichotomy between philosophy and poetry, between art and religion.

The integrating or synthetic view of art or poetry that he finds in Shelley and the Romantics, later became a central feature in Cousins' aesthetics. Cousins tries to explain the Shelleyan Aesthetics in the following terms :

> From ultimate powers inherent in the nature of the universe come impulses which, through the mutual co-operation of the intellectual and aesthetical capacities of humanity, fulfil themselves in the forms of the arts. These art forms, partaking at once of the nature of divinity which is their source, and of

humanity which is their instrument, are the mediators between both. Their capacity to act as such will increase through both the particular service of an illuminated criticism and the general advance of humanity in wisdom and altruism.[42]

This view of art as a mediator that Cousins found in Shelley was in fact first propounded by Schiller, the German romantic poet and aesthetician. Cousins accepts Schiller and Shelley's theory of the correspondence of the beautiful and the good, of the aesthetical and ethical. He also accepts their views in the divine function of art in the evolving life of man and that there is no dichotomy between poetry and philosophy, art and religion. We may accept these observations as the basis of Cousins' own aesthetics. We have noted earlier that Shelley was a rallying point for the late nineteenth century writers who tried to weave their spiritual aesthetics and radical ideas around Shelley's life and poetry. Cousins in this book has tried to establish the philosophic and theosophic nature of Shelley's thought. What he sought to recreate, is a kind of aesthetics which will celebrate a synthesis of intellect and intuition - divine inspiration and social commitment. As a literary critic and aesthetician Cousins carries on the spirit of the Romantic School. The German romantic aestheticians like Schelling, Schlegel, Adam Muller, Novalis and Karl Solger had a great impact on the English critics through the genius of Coleridge and Carlyle; Cousins' aesthetical view largely depended on these sources. It was those thinkers who had theorised about the concept of synthesis in the aesthetic context and Cousins' writings were based on the foundations laid by those German aestheticians who preached the fusion of poetry and philosophy, art and religion. Schlegel for instance, proclaimed the coming of the synthesis of poetry and science, the joint triumph of the Imagination and Intelligence, faculties to be reunited after separation of two thousand years.[43]

Cousins who followed the footsteps of these Romantic thinkers rightly called his book on aesthetics, *A Study in Synthesis* (1934). We have already mentioned earlier his synthetic approach to literature and art. This he has certainly derived from the

---

42. Chap. IV, Shelley's Aesthetic Ideals, pp. 83-84.
43. Gilbert and Herbert Kuhn : *A History of Aesthetics* (1956), p. 380.

Romantic aestheticians, according to whom the artist stands where idealism and realism, art and nature are united.[44]

The aesthetical application of this principle of *polarity* and dilectical union of opposites is the fundamental principle of Cousins' aesthetics. In the opening chapter of his book *A Study in Synthesis* Cousins takes his main objective as an attempt to resist disintegration of the human psyche which is a by-product of modern empirical and analytical philosophy :

> This, however, is due to the necessity of drawing the elaborations of thought, feeling and action from the analytical chaos into which they have been fragmented by uncritical "progress", back to their original simple synthesis.[45]

Cousins finds that this fragmentation of human thought, feeling and action are the root principles of the British empirical tradition. Like the German romantic thinkers Cousins envisages the emergence of a 'total Being' who would be the embodiment of a greater synthesis and would say:

> The expression of my religious nature is clarified by philosophy, and beautified by art. My philosophy is warmed by religion, ordered by art, assured by science. My art is enlarged by religion, deepened by philosophy, preserved from anarchy by science. And my science of life is made reverent, intelligent, beautiful by the rest.[46]

Cousins claims that this is the human expression of the attainment of wholeness or the unification of being, reflecting the unity of powers operating in the universe. He thinks that the fundamental human capacities are doing, feeling and thinking, and they are co-ordinated by a still deeper capacity which he calls 'intuition'.

Like the Romantics Cousins here speaks of integration and the means to achieve 'integration' or 'Synthesis' is the development of the power of 'Intuition'. Ages of human experiments through which human mind has been perfecting itself, Cousins seems to

---

44. Meyer : *A History of Modern Philosophy* (1966), p. 340.
45. Chap. 'The new Need of Synthesis', p. 21.
46. Chap. 'The Organum of Synthesis', p. 79.

argue, are making possible a richer intuitive grasp of the truth of things and therefore a more integrated form of awareness which the future poet and artist would apply.

Behind the acceptance of this integrative or synthetic approach to life and art is Cousins' denial of the separative principle or fragmentary views of life. He affirms that "In the separation life is dissipated; and no mechanical association can restore it. Intellectual analysis is divided synthesis. But synthesis is not added analysis...synthesis is primordial, essential, integral. It is not a condition to be attained : it is a fact of life to be realized and acted upon" (Preface, p. vii). By this synthesis 'is not meant mere eclecticism (a mere piecing together of things, even the best things)'. He observes "mere eclecticism can never be vital". Cousins wants that our human capacities "naturally become sympathetically orderly instead of analytically chaotic as it is at present". He says that "we shall not serve the purpose of life by merely lopping off the minor branches of our particular tree of life" (p. 31). His faith in this organic principle of life is in conformity with the Romantics and some modern thinkers like Whitehead and Aldous Huxley.

Whitehead in his *Science and the Modern World* (1925) affirms that nature is a living organism and he emphasizes the unity of all existence which was started much earlier by the idealist Philosophers and in England by Coleridge. The misconception which has haunted philosophy and literature throughout the centuries is the notion of 'independent existence'. Whitehead holds that there is no such mode of existence; every entity is only to be understood in terms of the way in which it is interwoven with the rest of the universe. Such thinking brings religion, art and philosophy closer to each other which is also Cousins' main objective: "In presenting that study I have given special attention to those elements in the human synthesis that are most neglected, religion and art;" ('Preface', p. vii). Cousins' thinking is matched by the theosophical claim of synthesizing religion with science. To him, the concept of synthesis is a firm bulwork against the dread of disintegration of modern life and culture.

Cousins, like the idealist philosophers envisages the development of creative life on the basis of synthesis of intellect and intuition. In *A Study in Synthesis* he carries on a protest against compartmentalization of knowledge asking tor "a synthesis of simple fundamentals of human endowments - intuition, emotion, cognition and action" (pp. 22-25). He claims that we cannot treat any of these as being completely separate from the others. "The same interaction" Cousins argues, "takes place in art and poetry proper". He, therefore, denies the contradiction between the objective and subjective, emotional and intellectual, realistic and idealistic in art and poetry proper.

According to Cousins art and poetry unify these seemingly opposed elements. Speaking about the role of intellectual or cognitive element in poetry he says that "the finest thinking in words, without the special poetical qualities of music, structure and figurativeness, does not make a poem".[47] But this does not mean undervaluing the cognitive element or intellectual element in a poem. What he wants to say is that cognition and intuition or intellect and emotion "must operate in unison"; for according to him "unemotional thought is ice, unthoughtful emotion is vapor" and "Art has no use for either" (p. 356). With this Cousins calls our attention to the unity of art and religion or poetry and philosophy. By Cousins' time the doctrine of the divorce of art from religion which had filtered down from the French Romantics (L'art pour L'art !) to the English aesthetes had taken on the form of proclamation of the independence of art from the realm of morality.[48]

As a corrective to this extreme views of the English aesthetes of the nineties Cousins offers his synthetic view of art and poetry. According to Cousins all theory that supports the maxim "art for art's sake" is grossly inadequate since it isolates the moment of aesthetic enjoyment from a more comprehensive sense of value. He thinks that poetry cannot retain its value if separated from philosophy. He says "when poetry is the projection of the creative impulse through high contemplation and intense emotion into strong and beautiful expression, it is not merely an utterer of the mental concepts that are the debris of concluded philosophical activity, but is *philosophy*.[49] Cousins hopes that poetry as

47. Chap. 'The Creative Synthesis', p. 143.
48. See Joseph Brennan : *Three Philosophical Novelists* (1964), Passim.
49. Chap. 'The Creative Synthesis', *A Study in Synthesis*, p. 158.

philosophy will bring a new harmony between experience and wisdom.

Like the Romantic aestheticians Cousins holds that philosophy and poetry, religion and art are co-related; and one should not see them as mutually exclusive but essentially related. Romanticism to Cousins was not merely a literary phenomenon but also very consciously a philosophical movement. The Romantics saw philosophy as an essential part of their literary endeavours. In romantic aesthetics poetry necessarily included philosophical thought; without it nothing truly valuable could be achieved. Frederick Schlegel says: "The whole history of modern poetry is a continuous commentary on a short text of philosophy: all art should become science, and science art. Poetry and philosophy should be united".[50] Novalis, the outstanding German poet and thinker, states categorically: "Without philosophy imperfect poet". Coleridge was thinking of this truth when he said that "no man was ever a great poet, without being at the same time a profound philosopher".[51] But being a sensible critic Cousins is quite aware of the danger of philosophy which deals with abstractions. Similarly mere versification of the sublimest truth is not necessarily poetry - "Poetry", he says, "must deal with thought as a vital process, not as a statement, as an act of creation, not as an answer to a sum".[52] It is therefore necessary, he says, that the thought which must be the hidden basis of the poem should be vitalized by feeling, and that be expressed musically. But even this will not make a poem. It must also possess the static qualities of sculpture and paint-ing, that is, it must show symmetry and embody itself in imagery. As poetry deals with the concrete, poets must give soul and body to abstractions. This statement of Cousins sounds imagistic but 'imagism' in Cousins' canon, is different from the notion of the Ima-gist poets. He says: "It is the intuition that come from the cosmic hinterland of life, and the formulation of these for interchange and the joy of realization through mental images, which constitutes the true imagism".[53] It is because of this

---

50. Siegbert Prawer, ed. *The Romantic Period of Germany*, London 1970, p. 305.
51. Quoted by Krishna Chaitanya in his *Sanskrit Poetics A Critical and comparative study*, Bombay, 1965. Chap. 'Aesthetics & Ethics', p. 253.
52. Chap. 'Philosophy & Poetry', *The Renaissance in India*, p. 213.
53. Chap. 6 'The New American Poetry', *Modern English Poetry*, p. 174.

philosophical attitude to Imagism that Cousins could not appreciate the poetry of Pound "after a dose of which", he says:

> One has a sensation of having been in some engine room where everything was moving and creaking, with whistles blowing, demons stoking the fires, and a mad-drunk engineer rushing about cursing the men in twenty different languages (pp. 174-75).

But Cousins changed his attitude to Pound when he read Pound's poem "Ballad for gloom" which he compares with a poem of Harindranath Chattopadhyay "The God of Warriors". Cousins draws our attention to the poem :

> For God, our God, is a gallant foe
> That playeth behind the veil.
> I have loved my God as a child at heart
> That seeketh deep bosoms for rest,
> I have loved my God as maid to man-
> but lo, this thing is best:
> To love your God as a gallant foe
> that plays behind the veil,
> To meet your God as a night winds meet
> beyond Arcturus' pale,
> I have played with God for a woman,
> I have staked with my God for truth,
> I have lost to my God as a man, clear-eyed-
> His dice be not of ruth.
> For I am made as naked blade
> But hear ye this thing in sooth:
> Who loseth to God as man to man
> Shall win at the turn of the game.
> I have drawn my blade where the lightnings meet,
> But the ending is the same:
> Who loseth to God as a sword blades lose
> Shall win at the end of the game.
> For God, our God, is a gallant foe
> that playeth behind the veil.

Whom God deigns not to overthrow
hath need of triple mail.[54]

Citing this poem of Pound, Cousins observes : "Here Mr. Pound touches the deep and permanent things of life and death, and - ceases to be a modern poet in the twisted modern sense : he becomes as old as Hindu philosophy in the subject of the verse, and as old as the English balladists (with some variation) in the form of the verse (p. 176)."

Pound's poem appeals to Cousins only because of its content which attains a synthesis of poetry and philosophy. Here Cousins thinks that "Pound becomes himself - not that grotesque shade that is evoked when people allow themselves to become the victims, instead of the masters, of schools and movements - he can show something of what the future poetry will achieve in virile thought, athletic feeling, and clear musical expression" (p. 175).

The apparently unrelated elements of philosophy and poetry are brought into mutual beneficient co-operation in Pound's poem and also in the poetry of the Indo-Anglian poets. According to Cousins future poetry would achieve this synthesis and for this kind of development in art and literature, Cousins thought the poets of India were making a contribution.

He says outright that in the West the rise of rationalistic thought has reached its extreme, in the denial of any connection between the artist and the philosopher. He further points out that such a divorce between the arts and religion philosophy and poetry is the natural development of the individualistic and materialistic character of the European thought. Aldous Huxley, the modern exponent of 'Perennial Philosophy' in whom the artist and the mystic are at war, naturally sought some kind of synthesis between the two. In his essay called "Art and Religion" he says: "Man is a whole, and so perhaps is society; but they are wholly divided, like ships into water tight compartments; on the one side of a bulkhead is art, on the other is religion". The road to health, therefore, is an attempt at wholeness to bring art, religion and philosophy close to each other and that is the faith in synthesis which Cousins sought to uphold. He says :

---

54. Chap. 6 'The New American Poetry'. *Modern English Poetry*, p. 175.

"Religion and art are, verily, the two highest and most closely related notes in the sestet of external human capacity. Neither can be fully itself without the other; and neither can usurp the place and function of the other without deprivation to both. Where art has been diverted into religious aesthetical formalism, it has become stereotyped and uncreative: where religion has ousted art it has become ugly and arid (pp. 71-72).

Though these reflections of Cousins are in close conformity with the Romantic aestheticians, he was no less influenced by some of his contemporaries, George Santayana (1869-1952), for instance. Cousins' Theosophic nature of aesthetic thinking found strong affinity in this American Platonist Philosopher and aesthetician who also believed in the synthesis of intuitive experiences in art. In his philosophy of art Santayana disregarded arbitrary distinction between morals and aesthetics and he described the arts as simultaneously useful and expressive acts. His significant work on aesthetics called *Poetry and Religion* (1900) seems to have influenced Cousins to frame his own views. Cousins mentions Santayana in his book *A Study in Synthesis*.[55]

The governing idea of this work of Santayana, as it has been explained by the author himself in the 'Preface', is that religion and poetry are identical in essence. In the final chapter of this book, "The Element and Function of Poetry" what Santayana states is quite similar to Cousins' views on art and religion or poetry and philosophy. Like Cousins, Santayana believes that poetry is "a glimpse of the divine and an incitation to a religious life". He says "the highest poetry, then, is not that of the versifiers, but that of the prophets, or of such poets as interpret verbally the visions which the prophets have rendered in action and sentiment rather than in adequate words. That the intuitions of religions are poetical, and that in such intuitions poetry has its ultimate function, are truths of which both religion and poetry become more conscious the more they advance in refinement and profundity".[56]

We are struck by the utmost similarity between Santayana and Cousins in their views of synthesis of religion and poetry. Santayana

55. Chap. 'The Creative Synthesis', pp. 157-159.
56. Chap. 'The Element and Function of Poetry', *Literary Criticism in America* (New York, 1957), Ed. Albert D. Van Nostrand, p. 309.

says: "Poetry raised to its highest power is then identical with religion grasped in its inmost truths; at their point of union both reach their utmost purity and beneficence, for then poetry loses its frivolity and ceases to demoralize, while religion surrenders its illusions and ceases to deceive (p. 213)."

Another book of Santayana, *Three Philosophical Poets* (1910) could have inspired Cousins to relate poetry with philosophy. Here Santayana considered three geniuses of world literature, Lucretius, Dante and Goethe. Each poet, says Santayana, presupposes a world view - a cosmology and a moral philosophy. It is this same turn of approach that we note in Cousins' treatment of poets, the criteria he demanded from a genuine poet are quite similar to these three great poets already claimed by Santayana. Cousins says speculating another development of future trends in poetry in his book *A Study in Synthesis* :

> For eight hundred years, there has been an oscillation of predominance between thought and feeling in English poetry. According to schedule we should now be moving towards thought after the Victorian and Georgian eras. But the schedule does not work. The poetical impulse is bewildered. Where it will move is not clear. It is, however, clear that an increasing intelligence in readers is demanding increased intelligence in poets and their poetry, and the spread of knowledge of physical and psychological science demands that the mentality of modern poetry shall be at the level of its era. On the other hand, there is an observable tendency towards the use of poetry as the medium of a finer expression of not only philosophy but science than prose attains. The hidden philosopher Robert Bridges ultimately found voice in *The Testament of Beauty* (1929) and Julian Huxley, the scientist, has taken to verse.[57]

This theosophical notion of unity of thought — Poetry, Philosophy, Religion and Science is behind Cousins' assumption. What attracted Cousins to this work of Bridges is the latter's elaborate attempt to fuse the Platonic concept of joy and peace in God with modern evolutionary thought of science. In Bridges and

57. Chap. 'The Creative Synthesis', p. 155.

Aldous Huxley Cousins observed a tendency towards the unity of intuition and speculation. They have inspired Cousins to speculate that poetry of the future would achieve a synthesis of intellect and intuition and science, philosophy and poetry would be integrated. This he has called a "Creative Synthesis". Here Cousins could have been influenced by the thoughts of Rudolf Steiner, the German anthroposophist, who also envisaged this synthesis of science, religion and art in his book called *Art in the Light of Mystery Wisdom*.[58]

On a broad view Theosophy is in essence an attempt towards this restoration of the 'Intuition' in our intellectual life. Madam Blavatsky who inspired both Rudolf Steiner and Cousins, calls intuition "the unerring guide of the seer" which should be developed because "through it (intuition) we are enabled to attain union with the superior intelligences".[59] Theosophy envisages that "All men are now at the dawn of a new age when they will pass to the new revelation of what Life is, as revealed by the Intuition. It is the artists who are to lead us into a new Eden".[60] Cousins' aesthetics is based on such assumptions.

Theosophy believes that Man is essentially a divine being and is composed of the High Triad of *Manas*, *Buddhi* and *Atma*. Manas or thinking capacity as some have supposed, is not the highest and best gift belonging to man. Its other, and in Theosophy higher, aspect is the intuitional, which knows, and does not depend on reason; the purely intellectual is thus distinct from intuitive knowledge which has affinity for the spiritual. Intellect, Theosophy argues, is not enough unless it is lighted up by intuition.

The complete trinity, Theosophists believe, is not yet achieved by man. When that will be accomplished the race would develop into a higher consciousness. Man has so far developed the physical, emotional and mental capacities - the summing up of which we normally consider as personality. But in addition to these there is another faculty which may be called Intuition which is necessary for the totality of being. In extolling this intuitive faculty as the best

58. See *Art in the Light of Mystery Wisdom* (London, 1935), pp. 197-198.
59. *Isis Unveiled*, Vol. I, p. 434.
60. See Jinarajadasa : 'Theosophy and Art' in *Life : More Life* (Adyar Theosophical Publishing House, Madras, India, 1934), p. 78.

means of achieving complete knowledge of reality Cousins, is therefore, affirming his theosophical doctrines. He devotes an entire chapter, "The Organum of Synthesis" to explain 'Intuition' as the main organ of synthesis.[61]

Cousins came to find that the dominant feature of Eastern thought is this insistence on creative intuition whereas the Western thought is generally characterised by a greater adherence to critical intelligence. What he sought in his theosophical aesthetics, was to bring the creative intuition of the Orient and the critical intelligence of the Occident into a synthesis. For a man like Cousins who has spent his whole mature life in India pursuing esoteric doctrines of Theosophy, nothing could have been of greater satisfaction than to weave out a philosophy of aesthetics where totality of his aspiration is embodied. Theosophy provided the vital impetus to the development of Cousins' aesthetics. He has made theosophical ideas more respectable by interpreting them in the light of German Idealism and contemporary Western thought. What he wanted to suggest is that religion and spiritual ideas propagated by Theosophy may be powerful sources of human motivation in science, art and religion and therefore have a far-reaching impact well beyond the sphere of religion narrowly defined.

---

61. Chap. II, pp. 22-80.

[illegible] Comte [illegible]

[illegible] achieving complete knowledge [illegible] Comte [illegible] theories affirming [illegible] [illegible] "The [illegible] positivism" [illegible] [illegible] [illegible] metaphysical [illegible]

Conclusions [illegible] that the [illegible] of Eastern [illegible] whereas the Western thought [illegible] greater adherence [illegible] intelligence. When he sought [illegible] the [illegible] was [illegible] [illegible] of the [illegible] [illegible] [illegible] spontaneous whole [illegible] doctrines [illegible] nothing could [illegible] [illegible] of his [illegible] in the development of Comte's [illegible]. He has made theoretical ideas more acceptable [illegible] What he wanted to suggest is that [illegible] and [illegible] [illegible] beyond the sphere of [illegible] defined.

CHAPTER - VI

THE RELEVANCE OF COUSINS

Cousins though not a major literary figure deserves to be remembered for more reasons than one. His life and works form a part of the pattern of East-West, or more precisely Indo-Irish, cultural interaction which became an interesting phenomenon during the closing decades of the nineteenth century. During this period most of the Irish Revivalists showed a keen interest in India and her culture. They turned towards India because of similarities they noticed in their social, cultural and political aspirations with those of India. They were in quest of a non-Anglo-saxon alignment and pre-christian spiritual values similar to those of their Celtic past and this they found in Indian thought. A strong feeling was cultivated among the Irish Revivalists that spiritually Ireland belonged to the East. Among the advanced Irish Revivalists Yeats and AE's interest in Indian thought was widely known. Charles Johnston (1867-1931), another key figure in the Dublin Theosophical Movement came to India by the end of the nineteenth century as a member of the Indian Civil Service. But he had to leave India because of his suspected political sympathies for Indian nationalists. His deep interest in Indian religious thought is revealed in various works he did after his retirement from India. His translation of the Shankara's Philosophy called *The Awakening of the Self* (1897), *Bhagwad Gita, the songs of the Master* (1908), and *The System of the Vedanta* (1912) were remarkable contributions to the study of Indian thought in the west.

The main channel of this Indo-Irish interaction was of course, the Dublin Theosophical Lodge, which was founded by a Bengali brahmin, Mohini Chatterjee in 1886. Yeats wrote in his *Autobiographies* about him thus :

> And we persuaded a Brahmin philosopher to come from London and stay for a few days with the only one among us

> who had rooms of his own. It was my first meeting with a philosophy that confirmed my vague speculations and seemed at once logical and boundless.

Mohini, 'the handsome young man with the typical face of Christ' later became the subject of one of Yeats' poems. Yeats' sympathy for India was further strengthened through his relationship with Tagore whom he introduced to the Western world in the beginning of the century. Tagore in his turn paid a great tribute to the Celtic tradition in his prosework *Pather Sanchaya (Easays and Letters,* 1939) in which he describes his meeting with W.B. Yeats. Tagore was also fascinated by the Irish mystic poet and social reformer AE, whose genuine interest in the Indo-Irish Socio cultural understanding is equally well known. In one of his letters written to an Indian correspondent on 17th Oct. 1922, AE says :

> I have watched with interest so far as I could the economic and spiritual movements in India, a country which I regard as a kind of spiritual fatherland and whose influence on the thought of the world must, I think, grow greater because in no literature is there such a reservoir of divine truth as in the Indian.[1]

What was much closer to Tagore's heart, was AE's ideas of Co-operation and nationality. Tagore was generous enough to own that AE's book on Co-operative philosophy, *The National Being* (1916) influenced his ideas on rural credit bank and Co-operative farming.[2] AE has also expressed his debt to Tagore. C.F. Andrews who interviewed AE in England in 1934 wrote about AE's interest in Tagore in an article, 'An Evening with AE'.[3] AE told Andrews that he was deeply inspired by Tagore's writings and specially by his philosophical prose work called *Sadhana (The Realisation of Life,* 1913). He said that this book gave him an outline of the philosophy of the East 'which he longed so much to understand'. Both Tagore and AE had a comprehensive world outlook. The spiritual regeneration of mankind rather than the narrow aggressive nationalism was their goals. The affinity of the Irish with the

1. Alan Denson, ed. *Letters From AE* (1961), p. 167.
2. Tagore, "Samabai Niti" (Principles of Co-operation), *Collected Works of Tagore* (Visva-Bharati, 1939-1948), Vol. 27, p. 481.
3. *The Visva-Bharati Quarterly,* Aug., 1935, pp. 91-92.

Indians seem so natural at a popular level that heroes like Tagore's Gora and Kipling's Kim[4] are presented with Irish connections. Gora, who turns out to be a Hindu revivalist was led towards universalism after his discovery that he was born of Irish parents who were killed in the war. Indian nationalism and Irish nationalism of the later phase were almost contemporaneous. The Home rule League of Annie Besant and Tilak was essentially inspired by the Irish Sinn Fein Movement. Margaret Noble, another Irish nationalist with the Sinn Fein connection made a considerable impact on the Indian Nationalist Movement in the beginning of this century.[5] She was a direct disciple of the great Indian Saint Swami Vivekananda and later came to be known as Sister Nivedita. Annie Besant and Sister Nivedita both of Irish descent, dedicated themselves to the cause of Indian nationalism and were widely respected all over India.

Cousins may be considered as one of this group of Irish expatriates working for the cultural resurgence of India. His life and work was a concrete embodiment of Irish-Indian understanding and their interdependence in efforts to create a new world of values based on spirituality and nationalism.

Cousins' coming to India in 1915 synchronises with the beginning of the Gandhian phase of the Nationalist movement. He saw India grow from the inception of the nationalist movement to the achievement of independence. it is therefore interesting to read his judgement on India after the post partition riots and culmination of it all in the assassination of Gandhi in 1948. Reacting to this brutal event Cousins writes in his autobiography :

> Unregenerate human nature asserted itself; and the dreams of a free country, remoulded "nearer to the heart's desire", turned into a succession of nightmares of murder and destruction and unspeakable misery, with world staggering assassination, on January 30, 1948, of Mahatma Gandhi, the apostle of non-violence ... That fanatical event was not a climax of evil but a symptom. The morale of a section of the people of the new Dominion of India fell to a low level. Happily the sordid

4. J. Mukherjee, "The Relevance of the Irish Spirit in Rudyard Kipling", *The Literary Criterion*, Vol. xxii, No. 4, 1987.
5. See Basu Sankari Prasad : *Lokmata Nivedita*, Calcutta, 1962 Passim.

stories in the press of corruption, hoarding and black marketing, and the dreadful list of wrecking of loaded trains with the cold-blooded killing and maiming of inoffensive women and children, has awakened the public mind to the need of a drastic reorganisation of life in such a manner as to allow the constructive and ideal elements in humanity to obtain ascendancy and control and a transforming influence over the destructive and material elements (pp. 768-769).

The India Cousins wanted to see and devoted his whole life to see coming into being, did not turn out to be close to his heart's desire. His shock at the consequence of the partition is a genuine one and every thoughtful Indian shares it. But in his true philosophic spirit he concluded with the hope that this was "the darkest hour before the dawn in the black and red struggle of humanity towards the light". He was not prepared to give up his hope.

Cousins lived in Independent India till 1956. He accepted India without any reservation and wanted to see India in her true self, a country which usually overwhelms Westerners. His admiration for India of course does not mean that he blindly accepted Casteism and communalism that are endemic in India. He fought against them as an educated Indian should throughout his forty years of life spent in India, a country which he called his 'Spiritual Home'. Cousins and his wife had close association with most of the Indian nationalists and eminent intellectuals of the country. They were loved and respected by Tagore, Sri Aurobindo and Sarojini Naidu and many front rank Indian leaders of thought.

Cousins' involvement in the life and thoughts of India was total and unflagging. In the thirties when there was a great controversy about the acceptance of Tagore's 'Jana Gana Mana' as the national anthem Cousins wrote strongly in favour of it. As a patron of Indian art and artists Cousins' services also will be remembered; he brought into prominence many of the younger artists and promoted the idea of establishing an Indian Academy of Art.[6]

Cousins' contribution to the study of Indo-Anglian literature is of considerable importance. The word 'Indo-Anglian' was first

---

6. See Prof. Binoybhusan Rakshit : 'The Need for an All-India Academy of Arts and Letters', *Modern Review*, December, 1942, pp. 490-491.

used by him and he emphasized that Indian writers have a role to play in introducing a new spiritual note in the literature of the West.

Indo-Anglian literature has not come into some recognition as an independent entity and its history should have an honoured position for Cousins. Criticism of Indo-Anglian Poetry certainly begins with Cousins. His two critical books, *The Renaissance in India* and *Modern English Poetry* provide us with a background and a critical justification for giving special interest to the literature produced in English in India.

To be sure, Indo-Anglian literature is not born only in independent India as some critics tend to claim. R. Parthasarathi, for instance, in his introduction to the Oxford anthology, *Twentieth Century Indian Poets* (1976) claims :

> In examining the phenomenon of Indian verse in English one comes up, first of all, against the paradox that it did not seriously begin to exist till after the withdrawal of the British from India.[7]

Any knowledge of Cousins' work will make us challenge such claims Indo-Anglian verse began with resurgence of nationalist sentiments and Indian self-consciousness with Aurobindo, Tagore, Sarojini Naidu and others who wrote in pre-independent India. Cousins' exposition of the poetry of Rami Reddy, the Hindi poet, Iqbal, the famous Urdu poet and Puran Singh, the Sikh mystic poet, in his book *Samadarsana* (Chap-VI) are also of interest as it creates an extensive background of the spirit of Indo-Anglian literature. The idea that the Indians have something new to offer was affirmed strongly and pre-eminently by Cousins.

Cousins' own poetry now can also be studied in the light of the development of Indo-Anglian poetry. As we want to broaden the concept of Indo-Anglian poetry, a poet like Cousins who lived in India and became an Indian in every sense of the term can be

---

7. See Dr. D.K. Barua's review of Parthasarathi's book in *Gleanings*, a Journal published by English Department of Dibrugarh University Assam, India (1976-77), p. 119.

considered among Indo-Anglian poets.[8] In the same way as we are now prepared to admit Derozio (1809-1931) as an Indo-Anglian poet we may call Cousins an Indo-Anglian writer.

Cousins was a genuine poet and naturally responded to the Indian scene, Indian thought and Indian religion. His verse play *The King's Wife* has a relevance even now. This is a play on communal harmony on one hand, and of mystical vision versus crude materialism on the other. It's Mirabai theme is still popular in folk drama all over India at present.

But one should note that it is the personality of Cousins and his great organizing skill that probably played a greater role in establishing his reputation. In the thirties and forties of this century Cousins became one of the influential figures in India's public and cultural life. He was connected with a number of organizations in India. He had been a regular contributor to various national, cultural and literary journals published from India and he exerted all his energy to strengthen their voice. He took a leading part in various cultural, social movements in India. Alan Denson in his short biographical note on Cousins has rightly assessed the genius of Cousins when he said that Cousins' work reveals 'a mind and character which was heroic in its aspiration and range of activities'.[9]

Cousins' activities are a major contribution to the cultural history of resurgent India. He lived in India from 1915 to 1956 - the most strategic period in the development of Indian nationalist culture. He was associated with all its activities from the beginning to the end. Perhaps Cousins' life and work is best epitomized in a poem written in his old age, 'Three Irish Poets' (1946). After describing the deaths of his senior colleagues Yeats and AE, Cousins here exclaims about himself :

Where will he die, the third
Of that singing clan
Who heard the sacrificial word
That frees the soul of man;

---

8. That Cousins' deseves an honoured place in the niche of Indo-Anglian poetry is recognized by R.P.N. Sinha, see his *Indo-Anglian Poetry : Its Birth and Growth*, Delhi, 1987, p. 116.
9. Alan Denson: *Letters from AE* (1963), p. 248.

He who from golden stuff and silver thread
Through Celtic vision wrought
Vedantic thought ?[10]

Cousins' life and work are indeed a mosaic of Celtic sensibility and Indian thought. We should remember him as a part of our cultural history. His active involvement in every facet of the Indian awakening, his close friendship with some Indian nationalists and poets, his contribution to the development of Indian art and culture through his patronage of young painters, his formulation of the concept of Indo-Anglian Literature make him the most fruitful embodiment of East-West interaction.

10. Cousins, *Reflections Before Sunset & other Poems* (1946), pp. 36-37.

A BIBLIOGRAPHY

(Primary Sources)

Bibliography of James Henry Cousins

(Division of Cousins' Works in Groups, the year of Publication and their place of Publication)

Group A : Poetry

1. 1894 *Ben Madhigan and Other Poems,* Belfast, Marcus Ward & Co. Ltd.
2. 1897 *Legend of the Blemished King and Other Poems,* Dublin, Frankling Printed Works.
3. 1900 *The Voice of One,* London, T. Fisher Urwin.
4. 1906 *The Quest*, Dublin, Maunsel & Co. Printed at the Dublin University Press.
5. 1906 *The Quest* (Second Edition)
6. 1907 *The Awakening and Other Poems*, Dublin, Maunsel & Co.
7. 1908 *The Bell Branch,* Dublin, Maunsel & Co.
8. 1910 *The Bell Branch,* a new Edition by the same Publisher.
9. 1912 *Etain the Beloved and Other Poems,* Dublin, Maunsel & Co.
10. 1915 *Straight and Crooked*, London, Grant Richards, St. Martin Street, Lecelster Square.
11. 1917 *The Garland of Life - Poems of West and East*, Madras, Ganesh & Co.

12. 1919 *Ode to Truth*, Madras, Ganesh & Co.

13. 1919 *Moulted Feathers*, Madras, Ganesh & Co.

14. 1920 *Sea Change*, Madras, Ganesh & Co.

15. 1922 *Surya Gita (Sun Songs) together with second edition of the Garland of Life and Moulted Feathers*, Madras, Ganesh & Co.

16. 1925 *Forest Meditation and Other Poems*, Adyar, Madras, Theosophical Publishing House.

17. 1926 *Above the Rainbow and Other Poems*, Madras, Ganesh & Co.

18. 1926 *A Tibetan Banner*, Madras, Ganesh & Co.

19. 1928 *The Shrine and Other Poems*, Madras, Ganesh & Co,

20. 1929 *The Girdle / Poems*, Madras, Ganesh & Co,

21. 1932 *A Wandering Harp; Selected Poems*, New York, Roerich Museum Press.

22. 1934 *A Bardic Pilgrimage*, New York, Roerich Museum Press.

23. 1938. *The Oracle and Other Poems*, Madras, Ganesh & Co.

24. 1940 *Collected Poems* (1894-1940), Adyar, Madras, Kalakshetra.

25. 1946 *Reflection Before Sunset, Poems*, Madras,Kalakshetra.

26. 1949 *Twenty Four Sonnets*, Adyar, Madras, Kalakshetra.

Group B Drama

27. 1902 One act Plays { *The Sleep of the King* - Subsequently reprinted in *The Quest* (1906). First published in *United Irishman*, Vol. VII, No. 173 (21st June, 1902).

28. *The Racing Lug*, reprint, *Shama'a* January, 1923, Vol III, No. 4.

29. 1902 *Sold*, A Comedy in two Acts - *United Irishman*, 27tl December, 1902.

30. 1903 *The Sword of Dermot* (Play based on Celtic Myth consisting of three acts). Prose version of the play first published in the *United Irishman* (2nd May, 1903), p. 2. Poetic version of the text was first published in the *Shama'a*, July-October, No. 3 & 4, Vol. III, 1927.

31. 1919 *The King's Wife*, Madras, Ganesh & Co.

32. 1942 *The Hound of Uladh,* Adyar, Madras, Kalakshetra.

Group C (Interpretation of Celtic Myth)

33. 1912 *The Wisdom of the West : An Introduction to the Interpretative Study of Celtic Mythology,* London, Theosophical Publishing House, reprint under the title *Irish Mythology,* Gordon Press, U.S.A. 1990.

34. 1925 'The Story of Etain : A Celtic Myth and an Interpretation' (Pamphlet) reprint from *Theosophy in Ireland,* May. According to Alan Denson Copies of this pamphlet are available in the National Library of Ireland and the Library of Trinity College, Dublin.

Group D (Literary Criticism)

35. 1917 *New Ways in English Literature,* Madras, Ganesh & Co.

36. 1918 *The Renaissance in India*, Madras, Ganesh & Co. The book is useful for those who look for a full view of India's cultural and artistic developments in the earlier part of the century.

37. 1919 *New Ways in English Literature,* Madras, 2nd and revised edition, Ganesh & Co.

38. 1919 *Footsteps of Freedom, Essays,* Madras, Ganesh & Co.

39. 1920 'The Creation of a National Theatre : a Chapter in recent Literary History' (Essay), *New India,* September, October, November, 1920.

40. 1921 *Modern English Poetry : Its Characteristics and Tendencies,* The Keiogi Juku University, Tokyo, Public Lectures in Literature, Autumn, 1919, Madras, Ganesh & Co. reprint Faulcraft Publishing Co. U.S.A., 1986.

41. 1922 Tagore's Message to the World. As proclaimed in his latest book 'Creative Unity' (Essay), *Modern Review*, July.

42. 1923 'Poetry and World Problems' (Essay), *Visva-Bharati Quarterly*, April.

43. 1933 'Shelley's Aesthetic Philosophy' (Essay), *Modern Review*, January.

44. 1933 *Work Promethean : Interpretation and Application of Shelley's Poetry*, Madras, Ganesh & Co. The book has been reprinted by the American Publishing Co. Vennikat Assoe. Faculty Press in 1989.

45. 1941 'The Poet in Philosophy and Affairs' (Essay), *Visva-Bharati Quarterly*, Tagore's Birthday Number, May-October.

46. 1941 'Substance in Swinburne' (Essay), *Prabuddha Bharata*, November & December Vol. XLVI, pp. 506-509, 544-552.

47. 1946. 'Literature and Occultism' (Essay), *Theosophist*, February Vol. 13 (This essay contains Cousins' analysis of Yeats'. 'Per Amica Silentia Lunae'.

48. 1946 'Tagore on Tagore' (Essay) in *Gurudev Tagore*, ed. R. Narasimhan, Bombay , Hind Kitabisthan Ltd.

Group E (Essays on Aesthetics, Paintings and Culture)

49. 1916 'The Art of the East' a Leaflet published from Madras.

50. 1920 'The Symbol and Metaphor in Art', (Essay), *Shama'a* (the opening number) Vol. 1, No. I.

51. 1922 *The Cultural Unity of Asia : A Study of the Tendency to unification in Asian Cultural Movements*, Adyar, Theosophical Publishing House. The book was dedicated to Tagore, the founder and the staff and students of the International University (Visva-Bharati). The bibliography Cousins presents at the end of the book shows his wide range of studies in Oriental religion and Culture. The concluding chapter is entitled

'India, the Mother of Asian Culture'. Part of this book was first published in *New India,* 31st December, 1922.

52. 1922 *Work and Worship : Essay on Culture and Creative Art,* Madras, Ganesh & Co.

53. 1922 'Modern Movements in Japanese Painting' (Essay), *Shama'a*, October.

54, 1923 'Japanese Culture, New and Old; Some personal experiences' (Essay), *Shama'a*, April, p. 151.

55. 1923 'Indian Academy of Art, Note and Comments', *Shama'a*, October, pp. 64-65.

56. 1924 'Vision and Utterance : An outline for the study of Relationship between mysticism and symbolism' (Essay). The substance of a lecture in the Arts Section of the Brahmavidyashrama, Adyar, Madras. *Shama'a* January, 1924, Vol. IV, No. 2.

57. 1924 'The Future of Indian Art' (Essay), *Rupam* No. 17, January, pp. 43-48.

58. 1925 *The Philosophy of Beauty, Western Survey and a Eastern Contribution,* Adyar, Theosophical Publishing House.

59. 1926 *The Great Theosophist Painter Jean Delville and Niocholas Roerich,* Madras, Ganesh & Co.

60. 1926 'Oriental Culture and World Renaissance' (Essay), *The New Orient,* U.S.A., Vol. III, July, No. 2.

61. 1927 'The Art Revival in India', Notes and Comments, *Shama'a*, April, pp. 133-134.

62. 1928 *'The Path to Peace : an Essay on Cultural Interchange and India's contribution thereto with a preferatory note on Mother India'*, Madras, Ganesh & Co.

63. 1935 'Art and Education' (Essay), *Visva-Bharati Quarterly,* May.

64. 1938 'The Fulfilment of Beauty' (Essay), *Prabuddha Bharata,* Setpember.

65. 1941 *The Faith of the Artist,* Madras, Kalakshetra.

66. 1942 'The Search for Perfection' (Essay), *Visva-Bharati Quarterly Abanindranath Number,* May-October.

67. 1944 *The Aesthetical Necessity in Life,* Madras University George Stanley Lectures, Allahabad, Kitabisthan.

68. 1948 'The Arts and Crafts of Travancore' (Essay) Reprinted in *The Arts and Crafts of Kerala* by Stella Kramrisch and Others, Cochin, Parico, 1970.

Group F (Essays on Philosophy and Religion)

69. 1913 *The Bases of Theosophy : A study on Fundamentals, Philosophical, Psychological, Practical,* Adyar, Madras, Theosophical Publishing House.

70. 1914 'War a Theosophical View' Leaflet, London Theosophical Publishing House.

71. 1918 'The Agamas of the Future' (Essay), *Modern Review*, February, Vol. 23, No. 2.

72. 1925 *Samadarsana (Synthetic Vision) : A Study in Indian Psychology,* Madras, Ganesh & Co. It contains an interesting Chapter on modern Indian poetry and showing Cousins' concern to bring out an anthology of Indian poetry in English.

73. 1925 *Heathen Essays, Essays on Philosophy and Religion*, An Examination from the Asian point of view, of the assumptions of "Christian Civilization" as to its superiority, finality and exclusive and universal efficacy.

74. 1927 'The Taoist Way to Wisdom : A Study in Chinese Philosophy' (Essay), *Shama'a*, April, pp. 83-88.

75. 1934 *A Study in Synthesis : Essays on Philosophy, Religion and Art and Education,* Madras, Ganesh & Co.

Group G (Essays on Reform and Education)

76. 1910 'The Philosophic Basis of Food Reform' (Essay), Subsequently Published in *Footsteps of Freedom* (1919), Madras, Ganesh & Co.

77. 1917 *The Kingdom of Youth (Essays Towards National Education)*, Madras, Ganesh & Co.

78. 1918 *The Renaissance in India : A Survey of the Chief Cultural influence in Modern India,* Madras, Ganesh & Co.

79. 1929 'University and the Future' (Essay), *Calcutta Review.*

80. 1945 'How the Academy Idea came' (Essay), *Visva-Bharati Quarterly,* August-October, p. 108.

81. 1951 'Culture and National Renaissance' (Essay), *Visva-Bharati Quarterly,* November also January, 1952.

Group H (Autobiographical)

82. 1929 'Musings on Life and Literature', a series of articles under the same title published in *To-morrow : A monthly journal of the New Spirit in Education and Citizenship,* Madras, Vol. I, Nos. 1-11.

83. 1929 *New Japan and its Impressions,* Madras, Ganesh & Co. The book is a travelogue but relevant to understand Cousins' observation on Japanese life, art and culture. Japan at this time attracted the attention of most of the eminent Indians, Tagore for instance.

84. 1950 *We Two Together,* Madras, Ganesh & Co.

Edited Works, Translations and Introductions

Acharya Raghuthama : *The Philosophy of Art* (Madras, 1929). With an introduction by James H. Cousins.

Basu, Phanindranath : *Principles of Indian Shilpashastra,* Visva-Bharati, 1926. With a foreward by James H. Cousins.

Bose, Abinas : *Three Mystic Poets : A Study of W.B. Yeats, AE and Rabindranath Tagore*, (Kolhapur, 1945). With an introduction by Dr. James H. Cousins.

Cousins J.H. (Ed) : *The Annie Besant Centenary Book* (1847-1947) Adyar, Besant Centenary Celebration Commmittee, Madras, Kalakshetra, 1947.

Ganguly, O.C. (Ed) : *Modern Indian Artist,* "Asit Haldar", Vol. 2 (Calcutta, 1924). With an introduction by James H. Cousins,

Khabardar, F.A. : *The Silken Tassel* (Poems), (Adyar Theosophical Publishing House, Madras, 1918). With an introduction by James H. Cousins.

Mac Carthy, Maud : 'The Holy Body' (Poems) with an Introductory Note by James H. Cousins, *Modern Review*, February, 1936. Another long review article on this Irish Poetess was published in *The Modern Review*, April, 1936, pp. 373-84.

Desai, Kanu : *Kanu Desai's Paintings in Watercolour*, (Bombay, 1938) With an introduction by Kulapati Dr. J.H. Cousins.

Richard Paul : *The Scourge of Christ*, Madras, Ganesh & Co. Translated from the French by James H. Cousins.

Reddi Rami D. : *Voice of the Reed (Poems)* (Madras, Ganesh & Co. 1924) With a Foreward by Jamesh H. Cousins.

Some Articles and reviews on Cousins' Works

Anon : 'James H. Cousins' (For this biographical sketch of Cousins, see Editor's Notes and Comments, *Shama'a*, July, 1923, pp. 258-261.

Besant, Annie : An appreciative note on 'James Cousins' by Besant published in the *New India*, 21 March, 1925.

Ganguly, O.C. : 'Dr. Jamesh H. Cousins : An Obituary Tribute', *Modern Review*, March, 1956, p. 221.

Lander Eveline : 'The Writings of James H. Cousins', *Theosophist*, Vol. 30. No. 12 (Sept. 1909).

Speight, E.E. : 'Mr. Cousins as Poet and Critic', *Mita Hyoron* (Tokyo) July, 1919.

Speight, E.E. : 'The Art of James H. Cousins', *The Japan Advertiser* (Tokyo), March, 1920.

Satya-Kantha : 'Dr. James H. Cousins', *Indian Educator* (Madras), Vol. I, No. V, 1925.

Unsigned Article : 'Dr. James H. Cousins : A Tribute', *Swatantra* (Madras), 17th July, 1948, Vol. 3, No. 23.

Review Articles

Aurobindo, Sri : *New Ways in English Literature, Arya*, 1917.

Biggar, F.J. : *Ben Madhigan and Other Poems, Ulster Journal of Archaeology* (Belfast), Vol. 1, Part 1, September (1894), p. 76.

Biggar, F.J. : *The Legend of the Blemished King and Other Poems* by Cousins, *Ulster Journal of Archaeology,* Vol. 3, Part 4, July (1897), p. 279.

This book was also revised in *New India*, 10th July, 1915, p. 15, Col. 2 by Annie Besant & & Jinarajadasa.

Bertram, I.D. : *The Renaissanace in India, Britain and India,* Vol. I, No. 8 (Aug.-Sept.), 1920.

Crane, J. S. : *Straight and Crooked, The Irish Booklover* (London), Vol. 6, No. 10 (May, 1915).

Child, Harold : *Straight and crooked, Times Literary Supplement* (London) 'An Irish Poet', 10th June 1915, Col. 4, p. 192.

Douglas, James : *Etain the Beloved and Other Poems* by Cousins, *Times Literary Supplement* (London), 29th August, 1912, Col. 1, p. 337.

Holingworth, J.R.P. : *The King's Wife, Britain and India* (London), Vol. 1, No. 9 (Oct-Dec. 1920).

Keohler G. Thomas : *Etain the Beloved and Other Poems* by Cousins, *Sinn Fein* (Dublin), 23rd March (1912), p. 2, Cols. 3-4.

Manauman : *The Quest* by Cousins, *Hermes* (Dublin), No. 1, February (1907), pp. 31-32.

Mead, G.R.S. : *The Awakening and Other Poems* by Cousins, *The Theosophical Review* (London), Vol. XLII, No. 247, March, 1908, p. 85.

Maurice, A.C. : *Etain the Beloved and Other Poems* by Cousins, *Irish Review* (Dublin), Vol. 2, No. 17, July (1912), pp. 276-278.

Seuman O' Congaile : *The Quest* by Cousins, *Sinn Fein* (Dublin), 25th May (1907).

Stephens, James : *The Wisdom of the West : An introduction to the Interpretative Study of Irish Mythology* by Cousins, *Irish Review* (Dublin), Vol. 2, No. 14, April (1912), pp. 100-102.

Sen, Arun : *Modern Indian Artist, Rupam* (Calcutta), January, 1924.

Unsigned : *The Awakening and Others Poems* by Cousins, *The Irish Homestead* (Dublin), Vol. 15, No. 4, 25 January (1908), p. 77, Col. 2.

Unsigned : *The Garland of Life/Poems of East & West, Modern Review* (Calcutta), October, 1918.

Unsigned : *The Renaissance in India, Commonweal,* (Madras), Vol. 10, No. 243, August 1918.

Unsigned : *The Renaissance in India, Theosophist* (Madras), Vol. 409, Oct. 1918.

Unsigned : *The King's Wife, Commonweal,* Vol. II, No. 283, 30th May, 1919.

Unsigned : *Moulted Feathers, Times Literary Supplement,* 8th Dec. 1921, p. 831, Col. 2.

Unsigned : *Moulted Feathers, Commonweal,* Vol. 12, No. 300, 26th Sept. 1919, p. 206.

Unsigned : *Sea Change* by Cousins, *Times Literary Supplement,* 30th Dec, 1920, p. 894, Col. 4 and again 8th Dec, 1921, p. 831, Col. 2.

Unsigned : *Modern English Poetry : Its Characteristics and Tendencies, Tomorrow,* July, 1921 *New India,* 12th Nov. 1921, *Theosophist*, 4th January 1922.

Unsigned : *The Play of Brahma, Tomorrow*, Vol. I, No. 5, July 1921, *New India,* 9th July, 1921.

Unsigned : *The Cultural Unity of Asia, The Hindusthan Review* (Calcutta), Vol. XLVI, No. 274, 15th Oct, 1922.

Unsigned : *Surya Gita (Sun Songs) together with 2nd Edition of the Garland of Life and Moulted Feathers, Theosophist,* Vol. 43, No. 17, August, 1922.

Unsigned : *The Philosopohy of Beauty, The New Orient* (U.S.A.), July, 1926, p. 77.

Unsigned : *A Tibetan Banner, Above the Rainbow and Other Poems* by Cousins, *Shama'a* (Madras), Vol. VII, July-Oct. (1927).

Unsigned : *The Oracle and Other Poems, Madras Mail*, Sat., 28th May, 1938.

Unsigned : *The Collected Poems, The Hindu,* 27th Oct., 1940, *Theosophist,* Vol. 62, January, 1941.

Unsigned : *The Faith of the Artist, Theosophist,* Vol. 62, April, 1941.

Unsigned : *The Hound of Uladh : Two Plays in Verse, The Hindu,* 28th February, 1943.

Unsigned : *The Aesthetical Necessity in Life, The Hindu,* Sunday, 27th May, 1945.

Unsigned : *Reflection Before Sunset and Other Poems, The Hindu*, 20th July, 1947.

Unsigned : *Twenty Four Sonnets, Times Literary Supplement,* 3rd February, 1950, p. 79, Col. I.

(Secondary Sources)

Books with Important references to Cousins

Aiyar, Ramaswami P. : *Annie Besant* (New Delhi, 1963)

Aurobindo, Sri : *Renaissance in India* (Sri Aurobindo Ashram, Pondicherry, 1920)

— — *The Future Poetry* (Sri Aurobindo Ashram, Pondicherry, 1953)

— — *Views and Reviews* (Sri Aurobindo Ashram, Pondicherry), 4th Revised Edition

— — *Letters on Poetry, Literature and Art* (Sri Aurobindo Ashram, Pondicherry, India, 1972)

Boyd, E.A. : *Ireland's Literary Renaissance* (Dublin, Maunsel & Co., 1916)

Boyd, E.A. : *Contemporary Drama of Ireland* (Boston, 1917)

Bishop H. Donald (Ed.) : *Thinkers of the Indian Renaissance* (New Delhi, 1982)

Cooke, John (Ed) : *Dublin Book of Irish Verse* (1728-1909) (Dublin, 1909)

Clarke, Austin : *Celtic Twilight and the Nineties* (Dublin, Dolman Press, 1969)

Denson, Alan (Ed.) : *The Letters of AE* (New York, 1963)

Denson, Alan : *J.H. Cousins and M.E. Cousins, A Biobibliographical Survey* (Kendal, England, 1969)

Ellman, Richard : *James Joyce* (London, New York, 1959)

Fay, W.G. and Carswal, Catherine : *Autobiographical Record* (London, 1935)

Finneron, Richard, J. *Harper Jeorge Mills* and Murphy, M. Williams (Eds.) : *Letters to W.B. Yeats, Vol. I* (London, Macmillan, 1977)

Fannery, James W. : *W.B. Yeats and the Idea of a Theatre : The Early Abbey Theatre in Theory and Practice* (Yule University Press, 1976)

Gregory, Lady : *Our Irish Theatre* (London & New York, 1913)

Gilbert, Stuart (Ed.) : *Letters to James Joyce* (London, Faber & Faber, 1957) (The Editor in his 'notes' called Cousins 'an authority on Indian Art, see p. 391)

Gregory, Padraic (Ed.) : *Modern Anglo-Irish Verse : An Anthology, Selected from the works of some living Irish Poets* (London, 1919) (Six poems of Cousins are included.)

Ganguly, O.C. : *Bharater Silpa O Amar Katha (The Story of my life and Indian Art)*, Calcutta.

Hogan, Robert (Ed) : *Macmillan Dictionary of Irish Literature.* (U.S.A. 1979). The book does not provide much infcrmation of Cousins', published works.

Ayer, Subramanya S. : *The Autobiography of a Free Thinker* (Karnataka, 1978)

Jeffares, Norman A. : *Anglo-Irish Literature* (London Macmillan 1982) The book fails to give us correct information of Cousins' life and work. Jeffares does not know anything about Cost Consins since he left Ireland. His observation that Cousins 'lived in India from 1913' is not true.

Kennelly, Brendan (Ed) : *The Penguin Book of Irish Verse* (England, 1970)

Kotoky : *Indo-Anglian Poets* (Gauhati University, 1969)

Kain, M. Richard O Brien James H. : *George Russell (A.E.)* Bucknell University Press, The Irish Writers Service, London, 1976.

Maurice, Bourgeois : *John M. Synge and the Irish Theatre* (London, 1913).

Macdonagh, Thomas : *Literature in Ireland, Studies in Irish and Anglo-Irish* (London, 1916), (1923 Edition omitted Cousins' name and bibliography)

Malone, Andrew : *The Irish Drama* (London, 1929)

Macdonagh, Donagh & Robinson Lennox (Ed.) : *The Oxford Book of Irish Verse XVIII - XX Century* (Oxford, Clarendan Press, 1958)

Mitra, Sisir Kumar : *The Vision of India* (U.S.A., 1949)

Monro, Harold : *Contemporary Poets* (London, 1920)

Nicholson, D.H.S. & Lee, A.E. (Ed.) : *Oxford Book of Mystical Verse* (Oxford Clarendan Press, 1916)

Nethercott : *The Last Four Lives of Annie Besant* (Chicago University Press, 1963)

Naravane, V.S. : *Sarojini Naidu : An Introduction to her Life, Work and Poetry* (New Delhi, Orient Longman, 1980)

Narasimhan, R. (Ed.) : *Gurudev Tagore* (Bombay, Hindi Kitabisthan Ltd., 1946)

Perkins, David : *A History of Modern English Poetry* (Harvard U.P 1976)

Prasad, S.K. : *The Literary Criticism of Sri Aurobindo,* Patna, Bharati Bhawan, 1974.

Robinson, Lennox : *Ireland's Abbey Theatre : A History* (London 1951)

Sturgeon, Mary C. : *Studies of Contemporary Poets* (London, 1916) (Bibliography of Cousins is given at p. 434)

Sen, Prabodh Chandra : *Indian National Anthem* (Calcutta, 1949)

Weygandt, Correlius : *Irish Plays and Playwrights* (London & New York, 1913)

Wade, Allan (Ed.) : *The Letters of W.B. Yeats* (London, 1954)

Background Study

(Books on Theosophy and Theosophical background)

Blavatsky Helena P. : *Isis Unveiled : A Master key to the Mysteries of Ancient and Modern Science and Theology* (Vol. I and II), London, 1910.

Blavatsky Helena P. : *The key to Theosophy*, London & New York, 1893.

Blavatsky Helena P. : *The Secret Doctrine : The Synthesis of Science, Religion and Philosophy* (Vol. I and II), Point Loma, 1909.

Blavatsky Helena P. : *The Voice of Silence : Being Chosen Fragments from the book of the Golden Precepts,* California Theosophical University Press, 1971.

Besant, Annie : *The Ancient Wisdom : An outline of Theosophical Teachings,* Adyar Theosophical Publishing House, 1972.

Besant, Annie : *Esoteric Christianity or the lesser mysteries,* Adyar, Theosphical Publishing House, 1953.

Besant Annie : *An Autobiography*, Adyar, Kalakshetra.

Bechofer Roberts C.E. : *The Mysterious Madam, Helena Patrovna Blavatsky : The Life and Work of the founder of the T.S.*, New York, Brewer & Warren, 1931.

Besterman Theodore : *Mrs. Annie Besant : A Modern Prophet*, London, Kegan Paul, 1934.

Boller Paul Jr. : *American Transcendentalism 1830-1860*. New York, Putnam, 1974.

Braden Charles : *They also Believe : A Study of Modern American Cults and Minority Religious Movements*, New York, Macmillan, 1949.

Cleather, Alice : *H.P. Blavatsky : Her life and work for humanity*, Calcutta, Thacker Spink, 1922.

Campbell, Bruce F. : *Ancient Wisdom Revived : A History of the Theosophical Movement*, California, University of California Press, 1980.

Christy, Arthur : *The Orient in American Transcendentalism : A Study of Emerson, Thorean and Alcott*, New York, Columbia University Press, 1932.

Cousins, James H. : *The Bases of Theosophy, a study in fundamentals, philosophical, psychological, practical*, Theosophical Publishing House, 1913.

Eliade, Mircea : *A History of Religious Ideas* (translated from the French by Willard R. Trask), Chicago, The University Press, 1978.

Eliade, Mircea : *The Quest : History and Meaning in Religions*, Chicago, The University Press, 1969.

Farquhar, John N. : *Modern Religious Movements in India*, Delhi, Munshiram Manoharlal, 1967.

Fairchild, Hoxie Neale : *Religious Trends in English Poetry*, Vol. IV, *Christianity & Romanticism in the Victorian Era*, New York, Columbia University Press, 1962.

Heindel, Max : *Blavatsky and the Secret Doctrine*, California, Santa Monica de Vorss, 1972.

Hanson Virginia : *H.P. Blavatsky and the Secret Doctrine,* Adyar, Theosophical Publishing House, 1971.

Huxley, Aldous : *The Perennial Philosophy,* London, 1946.

Head, Joseph and S.L. Cranstone (eds.) : *Reincarnation in World Thought,* New York, Julian Press, 1967.

Jinarajdasa, C. (ed.) : *The Golden Book of the Theosophical Society,* Adyar, Theosophical Publishing House, 1925.

Judge, William Quan : *The Ocean of Theosophy,* first edition 1893, London, The Theosophical Company Ltd. reprint 3rd Indian Edition 1948, Theosophy Co. (India) Ltd., Bombay.

Judah J. Stillson : *The History and Philosophy of the Metaphysical Movements in America*, Philadelphia : Westminster, 1967.

Kuhn, Alvin Boyd : *Theosophy : A Modern Revival of Ancient Wisdom*, New York : Henry hott, 1930.

Kandinsky Wassiiy : *Concerning the Spiritual in Art,* New York, Wiltenborn, 1947.

Leedbeater, Charles W. : *The Masters and the Path,* Chicago Theosophical Press, 1925.

Maitland, Edward : *Anna Kingsford : Her life, letters, Diary and Work,* London, Watkins, 1913.

Mcintosh, Christopher : *Eliphas Levi and the French Occult Revival,* London, Rider, 1972.

Munik Gerrit : 'The Influence of H.P. Blavatsky on Modern Art' in *H.P. Blavatsky and Secret Doctrine,* ed. Virginia Hanson, Adyar, Theosopohical Publishing House, 1971, pp. 195-203.

Nethercott, Arthur H. : *The Last Four Lives of Annie Besant,* University of Chicago Press, 1963.

Nethercott, Arthur H. : *The First Five Lives of Annie Besant,* London, Hart Davis, 1960.

Nelson, Geoffrey : *Spiritualism and Society,* New York, Scheken, 1969.

Olcott, Henry S. : *Old Diary Leaves : The History of the Theosophical Society,* 6 Vols., Adyar, Theosophical Publishing House, 1972-1975.

Ryan, Charles J. : *H.P. Blavatsky and the Theosophical Movement,* California, Theosophical University Press, 1975.

Ransom, Josephine : *A Short History of the Theosophical Society,* Adyar, Theosophical Publishing House, 1938.

Radhakrishnan S. : *Eastern Religion and Western Thought,* Oxford Clarendon Press, 1939.

Spinks, Stephen G. : *Religion in Britain since 1900,* London, 1952.

Saurat, Devis : *Literature and Occult Tradition* (London, 1930) (provides excellent survey of Blavatsky's system)

Somervell, D.C. : *English Thought in the Nineteenth Century,* London, Matthew & Co. Ltd., 1957.

Sinnet, A.P. : *The Occult World,* London, Trubner & Co., 1881.

— — *Esoteric Buddhism,* London, 1883.

Sinnet, A.P. : *Incidents in the life of Madam Blavatsky*, London, 1913.

Shirley, Ralph : *Occultists and Mystics of all Ages* with a foreword by Leslie Shepherd, New York, University Books, 1972.

Steiner Rudolf : *Theosophy : An introduction to the supersensible knowledge of the world and the destination of man*, 18th ed. with additions, tr. and rev., London, Kegan Paul, Trubner & Co., 1922.

Steiner, Rudolf : *Art in the light of Ancient Wisdom,* London, 1935.

Tulloch, John : *Movements of Religious Thought in Britain during the nineteenth century,* with an introduction by A.C. Cheyne Leicester, The University Press, 1971.

Thakur, Shivesh Chandra (ed.) : *Philosophy and Psychical Research,* London, George Allen & Urwin, New York, Humanity Press, 1976.

Urquhart, W.S. : *Theosophy and Christian Thought,* London, James Clarke & Co. Ltd., 1922.

Williams, Gertrude M. : *The Passionate Pilgrim : A Life of Annie Besant,* London, John Hamilton, 1931.

Williams, Gertrude M. : *Priestess of the Occult : Madam Blavatsky,* New York, Knopf, 1946.

Zirkoff, Boris de (ed) : *H.P. Blavatsky : Collected Writings,* Vol. I - XV, Adyar, Theosophical Publishing House.

(Books on Celtic Revival or Irish Renaissance)

Arnold, Matthew : *On the Study of Celtic Literature* See *Matthew Arnold, Lectures and Essays in Criticism* ed. R.H. Super (The University of Michigan, 1962)

Boyd, Ernest Augustus : *Ireland's Literary Renaissance* (London and Dublin : Maunsel, New York : Lane 1916, revised Edition, New York : Knopf, 1922)

Boyd, Ernest Augustus : *Appreciations and Depreciations* (Dublin and London 1911)

— — — : *Contemporary Drama in Ireland* (Boston : Little Brown, 1917)

Bose, Abinas Chandra : *Three Mystic Poets : A Study of W.B. Yeats, AE and Rabindranath Tagore,* with an introduction by J.H. Cousins (Kolhapur, 1945)

Bachchan, Harbans Rai : *W.B. Yeats and Occultism : A Study of his works in relation to Indian Lore, the Cabbala, Swedenborg, Boehme and Theosophy* with a foreword by T.R. Henn (Delhi, Varanasi, Patna : Motilal Banarasidass, 1965)

Clarke Austin : *Celtic Twilight and the Nineties* (Dublin, Dolman Press, 1969)

Duffy, Sri Charles Gavan : *The Revival of Irish Literature,* London, Unwin, 1894.

Denson, Alan (Ed.) : *Letters from AE,* Selected and Edited by Alan Denson with a foreword by Dr. Monk Gibbon (London, New York, Toronoto, Abelard-Scheman, 1961)

Denson, Alan : *James and Margaret Cousins : A Bio-bibliographical Survey,* (Kendal, England, 1969)

Dillon, Myles : *Early Irish Literature* (Chicago : University of Chicago Press, 1948)

Eglinton, John : *A Memoir of AE,* London : The Macmillan Company, 1937.

— — — : *Irish Literary Portraits,* The Macmillan Company, 1935

Flower, Robin : *The Irish Tradition,* Oxford, Clarendan Press, First Edition 1947, reprint 1978.

Fermor, Arabella Una : *The Irish Dramatic Movement,* London, Matthew & Co. Ltd., 1939, reprint 1967.

Figgis, Darrell : *AE (George W. Russell) : A Study of a Man and a Nation* (Dublin and London : Maunsel, 1916)

Fay, Williams George and Carswell Catherine : *The Fays of the Abbey Theatre : An Autobiographical Record* (London : (Rich & Cowan : New York, Harcourt, Brace, 1935.

Gregory, Lady Isabella Augusta : *Our Irish Theatre : A Chapter of Autobiography* (London : Putnam, 1913).

Gibbon, Monk (Ed.) : *The Living Torch* (London, Macmillan, 1937)

Guha, Naresh : *W.B. Yeats, an Indian Approach,* Calcutta, Jadavpur University Press, 1968.

Hyde, Douglas : *A Literary History of Ireland from earliest times to the present day :* new ed. with introduction by Brain O. Chiv. London, Ernest Benn, New York, Bernes and Noble 1967.

Howarth, Herbert : *The Irish Writers, 1880-1940; Literature under Parnell's Star* (London, Rowliff, 1958)

Jackson, Holbrook : *The Eighteen Nineties,* Chap. 'The Discovery of the Celt' (New York Knopf, 1922)

Morris, Lloyd R. : *The Celtic Dawn : A Survey of the Renaissance of Ireland 1889-1916* (New York : Macmillan, 1917)

Moore, George : *Hail and Fairwell* (London : Heinemann;1 New York; Appleton, 3 Vols. 1911-1914, 1925 : London : Heinemann, 1933; Ebury Edition, 1936-1937) Vol. 1 : *Ave,* Vol. II : *Salve,* Vol. III : *Vale.*

Marcus, Phillip : *W.B. Yeats and the beginning of the Irish Renaissance,* Ithaca, Cornely University Press, 1970.

O'Connor, Frank : *A Short History of Irish Literature,* (New York, Capricon Books, 1968)

O'Faolain Sean : *The Irish* (London, First edition 1947, reprint 1969, 1980, Penguin Books)

Russell, George William (AE) : *The Candle of Vision : An Autobiography of a Mystic,* London, the Macmillan Co., 1938.

Skelton, R. and Saddlemyer, A.(ed.) : *World of W. B. Yeats : Essays in Perspective* (Dolmen Press Ltd., Dublin, 1965)

Summerfield, Henry : *That Myriad Minded Man : A Biography of George William Russell - AE* (Bucks, England, Colin Smythe, 1975)

Tynan, Catherine : *Twenty Five Years : Reminiscences,* (London, Smith Elder and Co., 1913)

Taylor, Geoffrey : *Irish Poets of the Nineteenth Century,* (London, Routledge & Kegan Paul, 1951)

Yeats, W.B. : *Autobiographies* (London, Macmillan, 1955)

Yeats, W.B. : *Essays and Introductions* (London, Macmillan, 1961)

Young, Ella : *Flowering Dusk,* New York : Longmans Green & Co., 1945.

Index

"WE TWO TOGETHER," 1913

AN IRISH POET IN NEW YORK, 1931-1932

A SUFFRAGETTE ADMIRES A VIEW, NEW YORK 1931

CONFERRING WITH TEACHERS, TRAVANCORE, 1938

7. ART ADVISER WITH ARTISTS. AHMEDABAD

"WE TWO TOGETHER," 1947. PHOTOGRAPH BY HIS HIGHNESS THE ELAYARAJA OF TRAVANCORE